Diver Below!

Diver Below!

The Complete Guide to Skin and Scuba Diving

by Hank and Shaney Frey

Foreword by Joseph B. MacInnis, M.D.   Drawings by Shaney Frey

COLLIER BOOKS
A Division of Macmillan Publishing Co., Inc.
NEW YORK
COLLIER MACMILLAN PUBLISHERS
LONDON

With our deepest love,
to Shaney's parents . . .
Lawrence and Rachel Sagle

Library of Congress Catalog Card Number: 69-14169

FIRST COLLIER BOOKS EDITION 1969

Fifth Printing 1979

Macmillan Publishing Co., Inc.
866 Third Avenue, New York, N.Y. 10022
Collier Macmillan Canada, Ltd.

Printed in the United States of America

ACKNOWLEDGMENTS

The authors wish to express their gratitude for the generous cooperation of those who contributed to *Diver Below*!

We are particularly grateful to Dr. Joe Mac Innis, Ocean Systems, Inc., who read the manuscript and wrote an unusual and exciting foreword. John and Joe Schuch, Cougar Sports, Bronx, New York, consulted with us about the latest advances in diving equipment. Paul Tzimoulis, Editor and Publisher of *Skin Diver Magazine*, provided us with many of his outstanding underwater photos and arranged for us to get numerous pictures from diving equipment and boat manufacturers. This was the fourth manuscript that Betty Welch typed for us on time and accurately.

Our author-editor relations with Collier Books have been very pleasant thanks to Howard Sandum and Malcolm McPherson. We thank Jeremiah Kaplan, President of Macmillan, and Julian Mueller, Editor-in-Chief of Harcourt Brace & World.

Our underwater photographer colleagues who contributed photographs include Mike de Camp, David Doubilet, George Field, Al Giddings, J. Barry Herron, John E. Hopkins, Owen Lee, Burt McNeely, Tom McQuarrie, Chuck Niklin, Coles Phinizy, Ade Rebikoff, and Joep Strolenberg. We also thank the manufacturers and distributors who provided photos. They are Birns and Sawyer Cine Equipment, Dacor Inc., Ehrenreich Photo-Optical Industries, Honeywell, Ikelite, Johnson Motors, Kenner Boats, Mako Products, Paillard Inc., Parkway Fabricators, Rebikoff Underwater Products, Seamless Rubber Co., Sekonic, Sportsways Inc., Uniroyal Inc., U.S. Divers Corp., and Voit Rubber Co.

Contents

Foreword

Florida Shelf—Colony I
Lat. 26° 45′ 13″ Long. 80° 01′ 37″
50 Feet Beneath the Sea
One Mile East of West Palm Beach

Excerpts from the log kept by Dr. Joseph B. MacInnis in the Hydrolab undersea habitat toward the end of a 50-hour, 50-foot dive, the first undersea living experiment and biological survey carried out off the Florida coast, May 4, 1968.

. . . I have just finished reading Hank and Shaney Frey's new book . . . What a wonderful introduction to this wonderful sport. . . .

I've known Hank for years now and always admired his deep grasp of all of the technical aspects of both sport and advanced diving. I was particularly impressed with his pioneering efforts in the design of the thermal suits during the U.S. Navy's SEALAB II project.

. . . As the Freys point out . . . there is no quick and easy way to dive like an expert . . . it takes hours of study and practice . . . but their new guide gives the reader a fine working outline of the basic essentials.

. . . The book is up to date in all respects and is a lodestone of diving information. Hank's specialty (among others) is underwater photography and so this section of the book is particularly informative. Shaney's interest in art shines through in the section on underwater painting. This is also one of the first diving books that describes how to make lovely and unique fish prints . . .

Our dive here will come to an end in a few hours. We'll emerge from our underwater house . . . surface . . . and almost immediately begin planning for the next experiment. There will be countless such dives to be made in the future. We'll need many young people with a career interest in the sea to man these underwater stations. They will also have to have a thorough background of diving experience . . .

. . . I am confident that the Freys' new book will start many divers off along the right path toward obtaining this background.

Dr. Joseph B. MacInnis
Medical Director
Ocean Systems Inc.
Consultant to U.S.N. SEALAB III

Introduction

Our planet is truly the water planet of our solar system. No other planet has such an abundance of water. Less than 30 percent of our world is dry land; the rest is covered by water—oceans, seas, lakes, and rivers. Along thousands of miles of seashore and riverbank millions ot people have been captivated by skin and scuba diving. They have discovered a wilderness that will whet the appetite of anyone who is adventurous and curious. There is bound to be something satisfying under the surface for everyone—the fish watcher, the hunter, the collector, the photographer, the enterprising, the bored, and the bold.

Regardless of your age, you can teach yourself to skin dive—or snorkel—by following the instructions in this book. However, you must have formal training for the more complicated sport of scuba diving. And there is still some question as to whether or not repeated exposure to breathing compressed air might have an adverse effect on the lungs of people less than 16 years of age. The upper age limit depends mostly on the individual's physical condition.

You are embarking on a totally new range of experiences when you learn to dive. One of the many benefits, whether you simply explore and observe, search for treasure, or become a talented underwater photographer, is that you will meet enthusiastic, sea-loving people from many nations and from all ethnic groups. For those of you who are young, this fascinating sport can possibly influence you to seek a career in one of the ocean sciences—a widely expanding and important field of endeavor.

Wherever the sport may lead you, wherever your interest may lie, if you are adventurous in spirit and curious by nature and wish to explore the last great unknown region of our planet, this book was written for you.

Hank and Shaney Frey

New York
1969

"Duke" Pontin glides downward toward a forest of antler coral off the Florida Keys. Well-designed skin diving equipment is your passport to underwater paradises such as this one.

Photo by Hank Frey

1 | Skin Diving Equipment

Imagine that you and your friends, brand-new skin divers all, are cruising out to the underwater park just off Key Largo, Florida. The captain of your chartered boat is a veteran diver and he fully understands your enthusiasm for this, your first skin diving vacation. Now he puts the motors in neutral and drops anchor near a shallow-water coral reef.

Eagerly, you put on your safety vest, mask, fins, and snorkel and check your underwater camera for the fifth time to be sure it is loaded. Down the ladder you go into the warm, salty water. As you wait by the ladder for your friends to join you, you have your first glimpse of the mountainous reefs, the forest of stately antler coral, and the delicate sea fans gently swaying. The water is so clean and clear that there appears to be nothing to support your weight— nothing to prevent you from falling 20 feet to the hard white sand in the valley between the reefs. It takes a moment to overcome this mild attack of vertigo.

Then your friends are beside you and are ready for the first brief venture into this awesome alien world. You breathe deeply, quietly dive beneath the surface, and kick down toward the sun-rippled sand.

What photos can be taken here! Fish of all descriptions—tiny, large and medium size, red, blue, yellow, and green—swarm around and over the color-splashed coral. You must go up for air, shattering your mirrored image as you break through the surface. Your friends are as excited and overwhelmed as you are. Again you enter the strangely crackling world. Hadn't you been told it is a silent world? Yet you hear constant snaps and clicks from all directions.

You see a parrotfish munching on a knob of coral and you move closer, slowly and smoothly, to take a picture. The fish accepts your presence with calm, even disdain, for no spearfishing is allowed here and the fish do not fear the divers who come to admire them. A pair of angelfish appear to pose politely for you. A tiny, jewel-toned fish, no larger than your little finger, charges at you from atop a small but handsome brain coral. That is his territory and he protects it fiercely. A flash of silver attracts your eye. A young barracuda, curious as a cat, has come to watch you. There is so much to see, so much that is strange and new to you that you have lost track of time. Even so, you are surprised when the captain signals that it is time to go. The hour is growing late and you must leave the sea and return to land. As you climb aboard, you find that you are pleasantly tired but still exhilarated by this day's diving. You are anxious to return tomorrow.

If you enjoy swimming and are curious to see what is beneath the surface, skin diving is the sport for you. Skin diving requires relatively little training, and the equipment is inexpensive. The basic equipment for skin diving in warm water consists of a mask, a snorkel, a pair of

Photo by Hank Frey

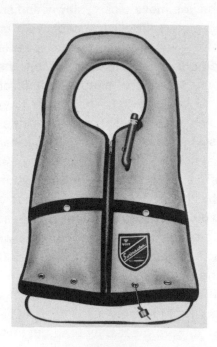

Basic skin diving equipment consists of a mask, a snorkel, fins, and the all-important safety vest.
Courtesy of Voit Rubber Company

fins, and a safety vest. It is worthwhile to purchase good equipment at the very beginning because good equipment will make it easier for you to learn the skin diving skills.

Mask

A mask allows you to see under water without blurred vision. There is a wide variety of masks to choose from, ranging from very simple ones to those with devices for helping you to equalize the pressure on your ears and to remove water that has leaked into the mask. It is a good idea to begin with a simple mask that is well designed. Later, you can use a more elaborate mask and keep the simple one for a spare.

There are certain features to look for in any mask. The faceplate should be made of safety glass. Ordinary glass faceplates can be dangerous, and plastic ones tend to become fogged quickly. The glass should be held in place with a stainless-steel band. The headstrap should be sturdy so that it will not break easily. Headstraps generally become brittle because of surface cracking due to ozone in the air. A sturdy headstrap will outlast a thin one. The mechanism for adjusting the length of the headstrap should be easy to use, but the strap should not be able to slip after you have made an adjustment. It is important that the skirt of the mask—or the part that comes in contact with your face—be comfortable and provide a leakproof seal. Masks made of hard rubber tend to be uncomfortable. Look for one made of fairly soft rubber—but not so soft that it will not hold its shape. Most masks employ the feather-edge seal principle. Some are fitted with a band of foam rubber to seal against your face. A well-designed mask using either type of seal will do.

Your mask must fit you well. There is a way, though not absolutely foolproof, to test a mask before you buy it. Without putting the headstrap around your head, hold the mask lightly against your face and inhale slightly through your nose.

Susan Young checks mask for proper fit and seal.
Photo by Hank Frey

The Vedo mask is among several designs for divers who must wear prescription lenses under water.
Courtesy Dacor Corporation

You can choose from a wide variety of masks. The two most important considerations are that your mask fit comfortably and that it be watertight.
Courtesy Skin Diver Magazine

A well-designed mask has sturdy headstraps, a stainless-steel band, and a safety-glass faceplate.
Photo by Hank Frey

Then, let go of the mask with your hand and see if it stays on. If it does not, it will not seal against water. If it does stay on, it will probably provide a good seal.

Optional features in masks include nose pinches to aid in equalizing the pressure on your eardrums and purge valves to assist in removing water from your mask. Nose pinches are worthwhile only if they are easily reached while you are using either a snorkel or a scuba regulator. There are two different types of purge valves: ones designed to remove a trickle of water from your mask and ones designed for purging your mask of water completely. Valves for purging small amounts of water are usually no more than half an inch in diameter. On occasion, this type of valve might leak if a particle of sand becomes entrapped in it. The larger valves are usually an inch in diameter.

Snorkel

A snorkel enables you to breathe through your mouth while your face is under water. With this rather simple device, you can swim lazily on the surface while viewing the underwater scene. The important features for a snorkel are a comfortable mouthpiece and construction for ease of breathing and ease of clearing water from the snorkel after you have dived. Do not look for a snorkel with fancy check valves supposedly to prevent water from entering. Valves on snorkels are not reliable under all diving conditions. A comfortable mouthpiece, preferably made of soft rubber, is essential because you can spend many hours per day skin diving. Ease of breathing is enhanced by a large snorkel diameter and a short tube length. The contours of the snorkel should be gradual; sharp corners make it difficult to clear the snorkel of water. The modified L-shape snorkel with a short tube is perhaps the best choice. If you plan to become a spearfisherman, you ought to choose a snorkel that has minimum drag.

Simple snorkels, without fancy check valves, are recommended. The snorkel should be flexible enough to prevent damage to your gums caused by sudden shocks.

Courtesy Dacor Corporation

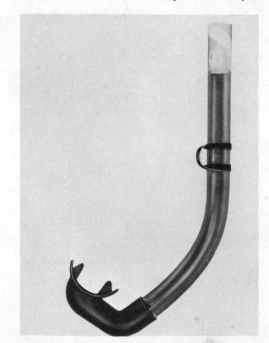

The modified L-shape snorkel with a short tube and minimum drag is a good choice for spearfishermen.
Courtesy U.S. Divers Company

Fins that fit comfortably will permit you to swim with increased efficiency.

Photo by Hank Frey

Fins

Fins permit you to swim with increased efficiency. You will be able to swim several times faster if you use fins, and, even at a slow pace, you will be able to swim with decreased effort. The most important thing to look for in a pair of fins is good fit. Fins that are too tight will cause cramps and will interfere with the circulation of blood in your feet. Fins that are too loose will cause blisters or will tend to fall off when you swim fast. Besides a good fit, you will have to decide on buoyant or nonbuoyant fins and on fins that have either straps or foot pockets.

Buoyant fins are more flexible than nonbuoyant ones and are accordingly kinder to your leg muscles. You should consider buoyant fins especially if you have not been taking the kind of physical exercise that strengthens leg muscles. Nonbuoyant fins are stiffer than buoyant fins. The stiffer fins generally allow you to develop greater swimming thrust. Some newcomers find it best to begin with buoyant fins and progress, after building up their leg muscles, to the nonbuoyant type.

Fins with heel straps are easier to wear with wet suits than those with full foot pockets. The heel straps provide a more positive clamping action than foot pockets. Foot pockets are useful if you plan to do most of your diving in warm water where you will not need insulated boots. They protect your feet from sea urchin spines, coral scrapes, and other hazards.

Safety Vest

A WELL-DESIGNED SAFETY VEST IS UNQUESTIONABLY THE MOST VITAL PIECE OF EQUIPMENT USED IN DIVING. WEAR YOUR SAFETY VEST EVERY TIME YOU DIVE. Although it is not a substitute for good swimming ability, your safety vest will be helpful whenever you get tired, and it will be indispensable in an emergency.

Susan Young demonstrates the inflation mechanism on one of the best safety vests money can buy. Note the whistle for attracting attention while on the surface.

Photo by Hank Frey

Reliable vests are made of rubber-impregnated fabric and are fitted with both a carbon dioxide (CO_2) cartridge device and a tube that can be inflated by mouth. The capacity of the CO_2 cartridge is important because it determines how much buoyancy will be provided to keep you afloat. A 16-ounce cartridge should be considered as minimum capacity. Excellent vests are available with fittings to accept either 19- or 25-ounce cartridges. These are used by Navy UDT (underwater demolition) teams.

You can use the mouth inflation tube whenever you would like to float restfully on the surface. Save the cartridge for an emergency.

Accessory Equipment

Diver's Flag

A diver's flag is not a basic piece of personal equipment, but every pair of buddy divers should have one. The diver's flag is essential to your safety. The orange-red flag with a white diagonal stripe is the signal to boatmen that there are divers below. Boats are required to remain at least 100 feet away from divers' flags. There are two ways to use the flag. You can fly it from a mast of your boat while you are diving or you can tow it with you. If you fly the flag from your boat, run it down as soon as you have finished each dive. If you tow it, fly the flag from a standard at least 3 feet high. The standard can be attached to a foam plastic float or to an inner tube.

First Aid Kit

A first aid kit should always be carried on your boat or kept handy on the beach. The kit should contain a mouth-to-mouth respiration tube, 4″ by 4″ compresses, gauze bandages, adhesive tape, tweezers, scissors, smelling salts, burn ointment, iodine or spray antiseptic, ammonia, eye wash, and an eye cup.

Keep suitable change—nickles, dimes, quarters—taped inside the kit with the phone num-

The diver's flag warns boatmen that there are divers below. It is essential to your safety.

Photo by Hank Frey

A knowledge of first aid and a well-supplied kit are important in case of emergencies.

bers of a local doctor, the hospital and the police department. It would be helpful to take a course with your future diving buddies in first aid and life saving. Then each of you will know exactly what to do in an emergency situation until professional help can take over.

Diver's Knife

A diver's knife is not a weapon. It is used as a tool to cut yourself free of any entanglement in the water and, sometimes, to clean fish. It is definitely not meant to be used Tarzan fashion—wrestling and supposedly subduing sharks, giant octopi, and the like. Your knife should be sturdy, should be made of stainless steel, and should have one smooth edge and one serrated edge.

Buoyant and nonbuoyant knives are available; both types have advantages and disadvantages. If a buoyant knife slips out of your hand, it rises to the surface, but a nonbuoyant one would sink to the bottom. Buoyant knives are slightly preferable for skin diving (because you are at the surface most of the time) and nonbuoyant knives for scuba diving (because you are near the bottom most of the time). Many of the really good knives happen to be nonbuoyant.

The best type of sheath for your knife is one designed to be strapped to your calf. Sheaths worn on belts around the waist tend to slip on the belt, making it difficult to locate your knife quickly. Worn on the calf, your knife will always be quickly available. If you decide to go on to scuba diving, you will find it convenient to tuck your snorkel under the straps on your sheath.

Weight Belt

You probably will not need a weight belt if you dive in warm water (without a wet suit). If you happen to be very buoyant, however, you may want to wear just enough weight so that when you dive you don't bob right back up to the surface. A weight belt becomes necessary when you wear a wet suit or parts of a wet suit.

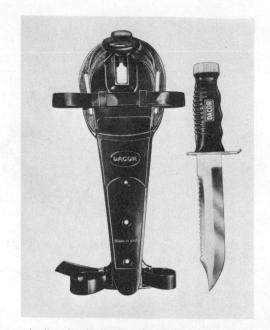

A good diver's knife is sturdy, made of stainless steel, has one serrated edge and one sharp edge, and has a sheath that can be worn on your calf.
Courtesy Dacor Corporation

The best place to carry your knife is strapped to your calf.

Photo by Hank Frey

The 2-inch nylon weight belt with a quick release is the most popular type.

Courtesy Sportsways, Inc.

Your weight belt must have a quick-release hitch, and you should be able to drop your belt quickly by using only one hand. However, the quick-release hitch should be designed so that it will not pop open by itself. If this happens, you will find yourself too buoyant to dive down to retrieve it. A 2-inch nylon belt will suffice for all purposes. Weights are available in a variety of sizes from 2 pounds to 10 pounds each. Lead weights designed so that they will not slide on your belt are preferred.

The amount of weight you need depends on your buoyancy and on the amount of protective clothing you wear. The average skin diver wearing a complete ¼-inch wet suit needs about 16 to 20 pounds of weight in salt water and several pounds less in fresh water. You require less weight when you use scuba and dive deeper, because water pressure reduces the buoyancy of your wet suit. You will have to do some experimenting to determine how much weight you require, because there are large variations among people and protective clothing. Do your experimenting in water shallow enough for you to stand up. Add weight to your belt until you sink slowly. Then remove weight so that you will be just slightly buoyant. If you do this in

salt water, remember that you will need less weight in fresh water, and vice versa. It will be helpful, for future reference, to keep a record of the weight required for the type of water in which you performed your test and the amount of protective clothing you wear.

Your weight belt must never be worn *under* anything—not under straps or shirts or wet suits, because if you got into trouble, you would still be struggling to remove the belt when you hit bottom.

Protective Clothing

"Protective clothing" includes anything from a T-shirt to a sweatshirt and socks to a neoprene wet suit—complete with jacket, pants, hood, mitts, and boots. What you wear depends on the temperature of the water and your susceptibility to coldness. You will find that you spend more time in the water when you are skin diving than you did when you were just a surface swimmer. And you lose body heat more rapidly in water than you do in air—about 25 times faster, in fact. When you get cold you begin to shiver, and shivering causes fatigue. Fatigue is an unsafe condition for anyone in the water. Unless you are diving in water at 75° Fahrenheit and above, you need more than your bathing suit to keep you warm.

As a rule of thumb, a snug sweatshirt and socks are enough to ward off the cold in water where the temperature ranges from about 65° to 75°. Some people are able to wear this amount of protection even in water at 60° if they are doing moderate work. A short-sleeve neoprene jacket is more comfortable and more efficient than a sweatshirt. When the water temperature is below 60°, a wet suit is a must.

The wet suit worn by almost all sport divers is a ¼-inch-thick foam neoprene suit. This thickness is usually adequate even in near-freezing water. However, you can spend less time in colder water. The closed-cell foam neoprene does not absorb water, and its tiny trapped-air spaces are excellent insulators and conserve body heat. Your suit should fit snugly to keep out large amounts of water; a little water will seep in under the suit but will be trapped and heated by your body.

A wet suit generally consists of five separate pieces: shirt, pants, hood, mitts, and boots. You might be comfortable wearing just the shirt in water temperature between 60° and 75°. When the water temperature is below 60° you will also need the pants and, most likely, the hood, mitts, and boots. You definitely need to wear the complete suit when the water is less than 50°. Be sure that the shirt has a high collar and that the hood extends at least an inch below the shoulder line. This double layer of neoprene protects the back of the neck and helps to prevent headaches caused by the cold. For the same reason the pants should extend well above your waist to protect your spine.

If you have trouble equalizing the pressure in your ears while wearing the hood, just pull the hood open a bit and let some water in. The water will be heated fairly quickly. Then you should be able to equalize the pressure without difficulty.

You have three alternatives in buying a wet

The "Farmer John" type of wet suit with one-piece pants and vest is ideal for cold water.
Courtesy Parkway Fabricators

Well suited and ready to dive.
Photo by Paul Tzimoulis, Skin Diver Magazine

Five-fingered gloves offer maximum finger dexterity and protection from cold water and sharp objects.
Courtesy Seamless Rubber Company

*A short-sleeve jacket with pants is sufficient protec-
tion for moderately cold water.*
                              Courtesy Parkway Fabricators

suit: custom-made suits, standard off-the-shelf suits, and do-it-yourself suit kits. It takes lots of know-how to make a suit that will last through the rigors of diving. Therefore, we recommend that you purchase either a custom-made suit or an off-the-shelf suit. The fit of a suit is important. One that is too tight will constrict your movements, cause cramps, and reduce the blood flow in your skin; one that is too loose will allow large amounts of cold water to enter the suit and chill you. Each part of your wet suit should fit snugly but not too tightly.

Neoprene suits lined with nylon are easy to put on and to take off, but you must use powder to put on suits that are not lined with nylon. Using powder can be awfully messy, and if you forget to take powder along, you will find it extremely difficult to put your suit on.

The most reliable zippers are nickel-plated ones. Other types of metal zippers tend to corrode more readily, and the teeth of nylon zippers break.

Dry suits are used by a handful of professional divers but, unless you go to extremes of care, seldom remain watertight. The wet suit is the best choice for recreational diving.

This youngster is among the millions of men, women, and children who share in the wonders of the under-sea world.

Photo by Hank Frey

2 | Skin Diving Techniques

Care of Equipment

Your skin diving equipment will serve you better and will last longer if you exert just a little effort to care for it. Most fresh water bodies contain enough minerals and contaminants to cause corrosion and the collection of bacteria. Therefore, it is just as important to wash your equipment after diving in fresh water as it is after diving in salt water.

Rinse your equipment thoroughly, using clean, fresh water. Allow it to dry before you store it. Check the blade of your knife from time to time. If it is dull, sharpen it. Check the cartridge inflation device on your safety vest periodically to be sure that it has not become corroded. (It will cost about a dollar to replace the cartridge.) Be especially sure to check the pull string, which tends to rot over a period of time and requires replacement.

Your wet suit will last longer if you store it in a plastic bag. Neoprene suits can be repaired easily by using neoprene cement. Brush some cement on each side of the tear, wait until the cement appears dull, and press the two pieces firmly together. It is best to wait for several hours before you use your suit but, in an emergency, you can use it within about 10 minutes.

As a skin diver you can swim lazily on the surface scanning the scene below, you can concentrate on studying the habits of the wildlife that particularly interests you, or you can struggle to haul a large speared fish 20 feet straight up to your boat. Anyone in reasonably good condition can swim lazily on the surface. However, you should be in peak physical form if you want to take part in more strenuous skin diving activities. It is not necessary for you to be a perfect physical specimen if you confine your activities according to common sense and to your own physical limitations.

If you are unsure of your state of health, consult your doctor. Making repeated breath-holding dives is hard work for an unconditioned diver. If you are strong and healthy, you will not be troubled by the extra effort. But if you have a respiratory or heart condition or an eye, ear, nose, or throat disorder, it might be aggravated by skin diving.

Swimming Ability

Competitive swimming form is not required for skin diving. However, you must be a competent enough swimmer to handle yourself well in the water. Test your ability by swimming 500 yards on the surface using any one stroke or combination of strokes. Swim 50 feet underwater. Then float or bob for an hour on the surface. Do all of this without skin diving equipment. If you do not succeed in doing these exercises the first time —or the second—practice until you can do them without fatigue.

Buddy System

Skin diving is a sport that can be enjoyed by men, women, and children—by entire families and groups of friends. This coincides nicely with the most important rule for all skin divers: *never dive alone.* Accidents happen most often to the lone swimmer on or under the surface. You and your buddy divers ought to learn from the very beginning to start out together and to stay together at all times. Youngsters must never be allowed to dive without an adult. The best way to instill this habit into your group is to learn the sport together.

Where to Learn

Decide whether you will teach yourselves how to skin dive or take lessons from an instructor. There are definite advantages in having an instructor. You will be assured of learning in a pool or in a safe body of open water. Some instructors supply equipment for their courses. You will learn to skin dive in an organized manner with your mistakes spotted quickly and corrected properly. And your instructor will tell you frankly when you are ready to venture out into open water on your own. Where do you find a qualified instructor? Inquire at a YMCA, sporting goods shop, or local diving club.

It is true that if you are all good swimmers you can teach yourselves. If that is your decision, then you must have access to a pool that allows the use of skin diving equipment or you must find clear shallow water that is free of boat traffic. Follow the instructions on the following pages and you are on your way to an exciting new experience.

Learning the Skills

The actual time spent learning to skin dive averages to about four hours. However, stretch this out over a period of days, about an hour a day. The very first thing to do is to put on your safety vest. You will then begin your first lesson with an unceremonious ritual that you will repeat before each skin diving jaunt. This ritual is called antifogging your mask. Dip your mask in the water. Then spit in it and rub the saliva (an effective wetting agent) thoroughly all over the inside surface of the faceplate. Dip the mask in the water again to rinse it off. This routine prevents the faceplate from fogging, which can ruin your underwater vision.

Snorkel Breathing

Put the mask on, making sure that you do not have hair caught under the rubber skirt, for an improper seal allows water to seep in. Now, slip the snorkel under the headstrap. Hold the prongs with your teeth and put your lips around the flange to form a seal. Stand in water about waist

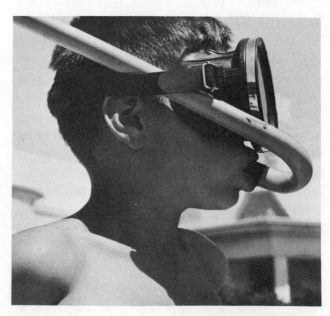

The mask and snorkel must be sealed properly to avoid unnecessary leakage of water.

Photo by Hank Frey

Take a deep breath and hold it. Dip your head far enough below the surface to let water enter the snorkel. Raise your head and, when the tip of the snorkel is out of the water, exhale forcefully.

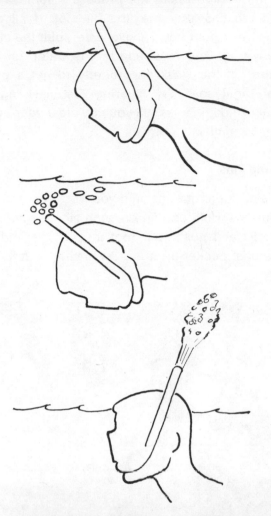

deep and bend over, putting your head in the water. Breathe only through your mouth until you feel confident that you are getting a normal supply of air through the snorkel. At this point, take a deep breath, hold it, and dip your head and the entire snorkel all the way under the surface. Do not worry about swallowing water. Air trapped in the snorkel tube will allow only a little water to enter through the top of the snorkel. Now, lift your head until the top of the snorkel is just above the surface. Exhale rapidly and with enough force to blow the water out of the snorkel. Resume normal breathing. Practice doing this until you know how forceful your exhalation must be in order to clear the snorkel. You will hear a gurgling sound if you have not cleared the snorkel completely. If this happens, take a slow breath to prevent sucking up the water. Then blow out again.

Exhale forcefully as though you were blowing out all the candles on a birthday cake.

Photo by Hank Frey

Clearing the Face Mask

Learn to clear your mask of water to prepare for the day when it becomes flooded accidentally. Put a finger under the skirt of the mask to allow water to enter. Let the mask fill at least halfway with water. Turn your head so that the side opposite the snorkel is downward. The mask must be completely underwater and the tip of the snorkel must be above water. Hold the uppermost side of the mask against your face and blow air through your nose into the mask. The air will force the water out of the lower part of the mask. Repeat the process if some water still remains after the first attempt. If all else fails, raise your head above water, pull the mask away from your face, and let the water run out. Then put the mask on properly to get a good watertight seal. Try clearing the mask again. Practice doing this until you can clear your mask without difficulty.

Using Fins

It is easier to put fins on if you wet your feet and your fins. Hold one fin on each side, using both hands, and push your foot into it. Then adjust the heel pocket or strap. Swimming with fins is

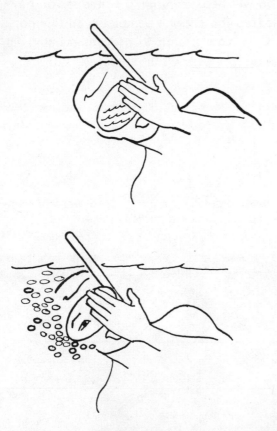

Press the uppermost side of the mask against your face. Take a deep breath and blow through your nose. Because air is lighter than water, air will occupy the uppermost volume in the mask and force the water downward. You may have to repeat this two or three times to remove most of the water from your mask.

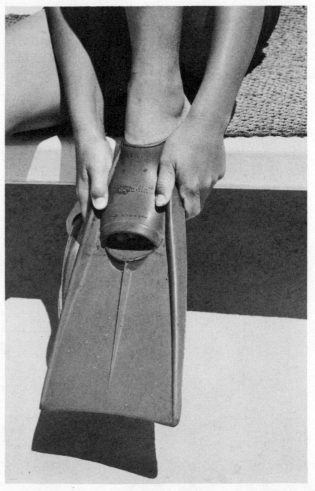

Hold your fin with both hands and push your foot into it.

Photo by Hank Frey

quite different from everyday surface swimming, and it may take a while for your leg muscles to become accustomed to swimming with flipper-like extensions on your feet. You will discover that you move quietly though powerfully through the water with fins. Keep your arms close to your sides unless you are carrying a camera or some other equipment. This position gives you a more streamlined, fishlike form and decreases drag.

Leg Kicks

The leg kicks used in skin diving are easy to master. The main thing to remember is that all movement should be smooth and rhythmic—no thrashing legs or fins splashing the surface. You are learning to skin dive so you can see the sights, explore the underwater world. You can do this successfully only by attracting as little attention to yourself as possible. You can adopt your own natural kick to swimming with fins or you can use either the flutter kick or the scissors kick.

The flutter kick can be a slow, easy kick. Move your legs from your hips in about a 2-foot arc with your knees bent slightly. Do this about 30 times per minute. Your fins should not break through the surface of the water.

The scissors kick will provide you with a change of pace during a long surface swim when your legs tend to grow tired. To do the scissors kick, roll over on your side and move your legs almost, but not quite, as though you were riding a bicycle. You can glide between scissors kicks.

Equalizing Ear Pressure

Before you go on to the next skin diving skill, it is necessary to stop and learn just a little about pressure beneath the surface. As you dive, the increased water pressure pushes against your body and raises the diaphragm just below your lungs. This, in turn, compresses the air in your lungs. The compressed air then exerts a pressure equal to the pressure of the surrounding water. This causes no sensation whatsoever except in your ears. Unless the compressed air in your lungs can travel up to your middle-ear spaces, the pressure in your middle-ear spaces will be less than the water pressure. This difference in pressure can cause severe discomfort, and, in the extreme case, your eardrums will rupture if you do not equalize the pressure.

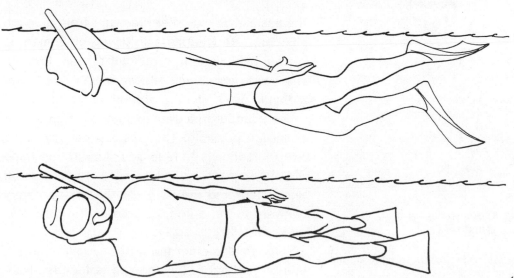

(top) The flutter kick.
(bottom) The scissors kick.

Equalizing the pressure in your ears would be no problem if the compressed air could travel easily to your middle ears. However, the Eustachian tubes, through which the air must travel, are small in diameter and are sometimes congested. You must help the air find its way through the Eustachian tubes. There are several ways to do this.

Start equalizing—or clearing—your ears as soon as you begin to dive from the surface. Press your mask against your face and exhale through your nose. You should hear a squeak or pop in your ears as your eardrums resume their equilibrium position. The discomfort will then disap-

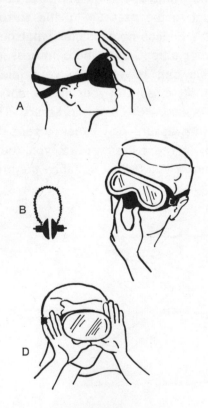

Methods of equalizing middle-ear pressure.
(a) Hold mask tightly against face.
(b) Use nose clip.
(c) Use nose-pinch mask (after learning with simple mask).
(d) Push skirt of mask upward to seal off nostrils.

pear. If you have difficulty, do not descend any farther. Ascend a few feet and try again. Clear your ears immediately at the first feeling of discomfort or pain.

Some masks feature a nose pinch. With such a mask, you just pinch your nostrils closed with your thumb and forefinger and then you blow against the closed nostrils. With other masks, use both thumbs to push the skirt of the mask up against your nostrils and then blow. Or you can push the mask against your face with just one hand and blow.

You might be able to clear your ears simply by yawning or by moving your jaws from side to side. Try all these methods and choose the one that is most comfortable for you. Remember, if your ears do not equalize, go up a few feet and try again.

Clearing your ears may be more difficult on some days than on others. This can be due to slight congestion or to cold water, which causes the Eustachian tubes to constrict. Never dive with a severe cold. Use nose drops or nose sprays only on rare occasions, because such drugs are dangerous when used frequently and over a prolonged period by skin divers.

Entering and Leaving the Water

The easiest way to enter the water from a beach while you are wearing skin diving equipment is to walk backward. It is difficult to walk forward with swim fins. Walk backward until the water is about knee high, turn around, and swim away.

Use a ladder in a swimming pool or on a boat whenever possible. The easiest way to climb down a ladder is to hold your fins in one hand and put them on in the water. Take your fins off before boarding the boat, for they make it very awkward to get a firm foothold on the rung of a ladder.

You can also enter the water by rolling off the side of the boat or by stepping in feetfirst. Rolling off the side is a handy way to enter from a

Look straight out toward the horizon, hold your mask and snorkel in place, take a breath, and step off.
Photo by Hank Frey

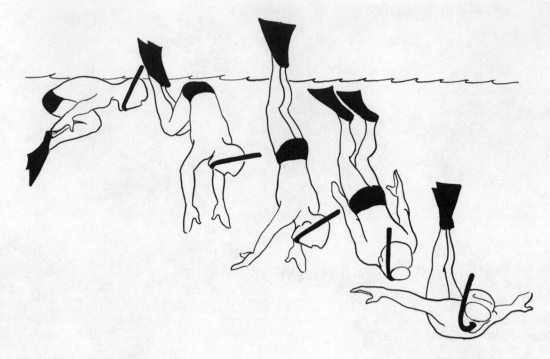

The tuck surface dive.

The pike surface dive.

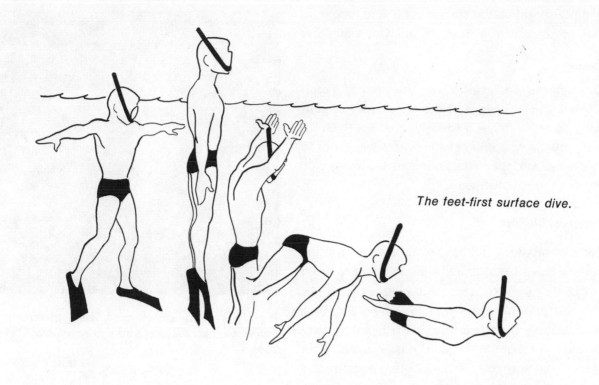

The feet-first surface dive.

small boat. Put your feet over the side, hold your mask and snorkel firmly in place with one hand, hold your breath, and roll sideways into the water. To step in feetfirst, look down to make sure it is safe, then look straight out toward the horizon, hold your mask and snorkel with one hand, hold your breath, and take a step as though you were beginning to walk away. Rise to the surface, clear your snorkel, and flutter-kick away.

Never dive headfirst when you wear a mask. If you do, the mask either will come off or be forced against your face with a strong impulse.

Surface Dives

As you swim along the surface, you will see many sights below that demand closer inspection. How do you get down there without a struggle and without scaring all the fish away? The following surface dives will get you there easily, gracefully, and quietly when executed properly.

Tuck

Tuck—or pull—your knees up to your chest. Hold your legs in that position and roll your body forward. Your head is now pointed toward the bottom. Straighten your legs so that they extend above the surface. The weight of your legs above water will push you down. Use your arms in a breast armstroke to give you added downward thrust. As soon as your fins are below the surface, begin to flutter-kick with your arms against your sides. When you begin your ascent, look up to avoid any obstacles (such as the bottom of your boat) in your way.

Pike

Bend your body at the hips. Keep your legs straight and bring them in line with your body.

Again use the breast armstroke and begin to kick as soon as your fins are below the surface.

Feetfirst

Kick up and push down with your hands simultaneously. The weight of the upper part of your body above water will force you down. Push up with your hands against the water as you drop below the surface. Then bend at the waist and begin to kick downward.

Hyperventilation

Hyperventilation means taking five or six extremely deep breaths just before a dive in order to exhale as much carbon dioxide as possible. It is possible to extend your breath-holding time considerably by doing this, but it is a very dangerous practice. You can easily upset your carbon dioxide/oxygen monitoring system and lapse into unconsciousness (see Chapter Three). Hyperventilation has no place in skin diving. Do not be tempted to extend your breath-holding time by hyperventilation because it can be, and has been, fatal.

Safety Rules

Always wear a safety vest.
Always dive with a buddy—and stay with him.
Tow a diver's flag and float.
Equalize your ears.
Look up as you ascend.
Never dive with a cold or when you are tired or sick.
Never hyperventilate.
Surface as soon as you feel the urge to breathe.

There are many sights to be seen in inland fresh water, such as these plants that resemble Christmas trees.

Photo by Hank Frey

The remains of a ship, resting in shallow water off Grand Cayman Island, are visited by a skin diving explorer.

Photo by Paul Tzimoulis, Skin Diver Magazine

There are many activities to pursue as a skin diver. Tom Hubbel has found his supper in the waters of the British West Indies.
Photo by Burton McNeely, Land O'Lakes, Florida

Skin and scuba diving differ from other sports in that they lead you into an altogether new environment.

Photo by Hank Frey

3 | You and the Environment

It is important that you learn how the underwater environment affects you so that you can enjoy its fascinations in safety. Admittedly, there are hazards every time you venture beneath the waves. The hazards are more severe and more numerous in scuba diving than in skin diving. However, if you take some very simple precautions and use common sense, you can avoid the dangers. Almost all diving accidents occur because of ignorance, recklessness, or panic.

The Environment

There is little difference in how your body is affected by salt water and by fresh water. The main differences between the two types of natural water bodies are their densities, salt content, currents, and such surface conditions as waves, swell, and surf.

Pressure

Perhaps the most noticeable difference between the atmosphere and the oceans (and fresh water bodies) is the way that pressure varies with height and depth. Pressure changes occur at a much greater rate in water than they do in air. Atmospheric pressure at the surface is the weight of air pressing against the earth's surface. Air may not seem very heavy, but the weight of a column of air that reaches the upper boundary of the atmosphere creates a pressure of 14.7 pounds per square inch at the earth's surface. (This is known as one atmosphere of pressure, or simply one atmosphere.)

The pressure at any depth in water is equal to the atmospheric pressure at the surface plus the pressure caused by the weight of the water. The pressure at 33 feet of sea water is equal to twice the pressure at the surface. In other words, it takes only 33 feet of sea water to equal the pressure caused by the entire atmosphere. The density (weight per volume) of fresh water is less than that of sea water; about 34 feet of fresh water is equivalent to one atmosphere of pressure. Every foot of sea water contributes 0.445 pounds per square inch of pressure, and every foot of fresh water contributes 0.434 pounds per square inch.

Pressure caused by the weight of water is known as hydrostatic pressure. Hydrostatic pressure at any point in the water exerts itself equally in all directions. It presses upward and sideways as well as downward.

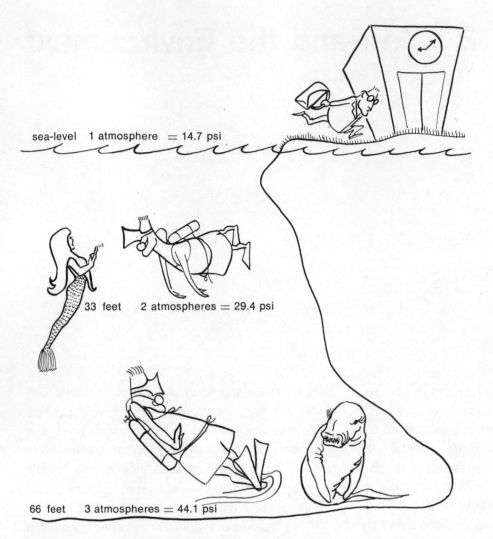

sea-level   1 atmosphere $=$ 14.7 psi

33 feet   2 atmospheres $=$ 29.4 psi

66 feet   3 atmospheres $=$ 44.1 psi

The pressure at any depth in water is equal to the atmospheric pressure at the surface plus the pressure caused by the weight of the water.

Compressible objects change volume because of varying pressure. The largest volume variations occur near the surface. This fact is particularly important in scuba diving.

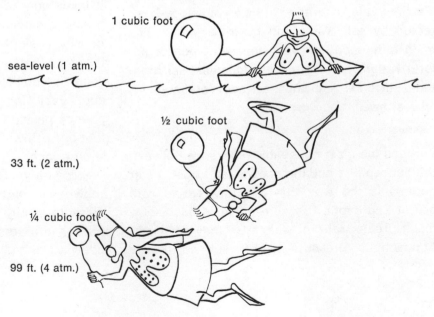

1 cubic foot

sea-level (1 atm.)

½ cubic foot

33 ft. (2 atm.)

¼ cubic foot

99 ft. (4 atm.)

The sinuses.

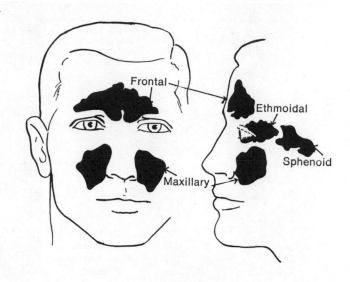

Volume Variations

Compressible objects change volume because of varying pressure. They become smaller and smaller as the depth is increased. The relationship between pressure and volume is simple. Volume varies inversely with the absolute pressure (atmospheric pressure plus hydrostatic pressure). For example, suppose that a balloon containing air at the surface is lowered 33 feet into the sea. At this depth it will be subjected to two atmospheres of absolute pressure and its volume will be one-half of its volume at the surface. At three atmospheres absolute (66 feet), it will be one-third its original size. It will be one-fourth the size at four atmospheres absolute (99 feet) and one-fifth the size at five atmospheres absolute (132 feet), and so on.

The largest volume changes occur near the surface. The volume is reduced by one-half in the first 33 feet of water. However, to reduce the volume again by one-half the compressible object must be lowered to 99 feet—a difference of 66 feet. This fact is particularly important in scuba diving, as you shall see in the section on air embolism and related accidents. It is also important in skin diving because it can result, at great enough depths, in lung squeeze.

Fortunately, your body is virtually incompressible except for your lungs, airways, and sinuses. You do not actually notice pressure, except on your eardrums, because it is equalized by the pressure within your compressible cavities and because your flesh and bones are almost completely incompressible.

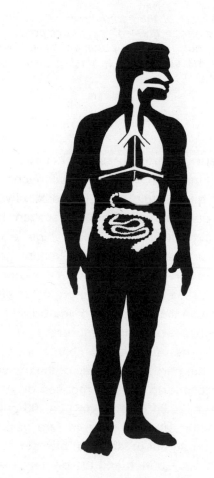

Air spaces in the human body (middle-ear and sinus spaces not shown).

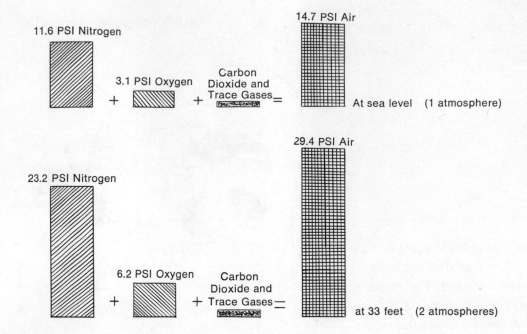

11.6 PSI Nitrogen

3.1 PSI Oxygen

+

Carbon
Dioxide and
Trace Gases

+

=

14.7 PSI Air

At sea level   (1 atmosphere)

23.2 PSI Nitrogen

6.2 PSI Oxygen

+

Carbon
Dioxide and
Trace Gases

+

—

29.4 PSI Air

at 33 feet   (2 atmospheres)

Partial pressures of the components of air. The percentage—or proportion—of each component does not change, but its partial pressure does. The total pressure is the sum of the partial pressure of the gases present.

Partial Pressure

The concept of partial pressure is important in understanding how the individual gases in a mixture of gases affect you. Paradoxically oxygen—the one gas essential to sustain life—becomes extremely toxic under high enough pressure. Nitrogen, the most abundant gas in air, causes a sort of narcosis when it is breathed under high pressure. And there are other effects that depend on the pressures of individual gases—their so-called partial pressures.

The total pressure of a gas mixture is equal to the sum of the partial pressures of the individual gases. Atmospheric air is composed of 79 percent nitrogen, 20.94 percent oxygen, .03 percent carbon dioxide, and .03 percent rare gases. At sea level, the partial pressure of nitrogen is 11.6 pounds per square inch and the partial pressure of oxygen is 3.1 pounds per square inch. These figures double at 33 feet in the ocean and they triple at 66 feet of depth.

The rate at which your body tissues absorb gas is proportional to the partial pressure of the gas. This has direct bearing on some of the hazards discussed later in this chapter.

Buoyancy

The density of water plays a leading role in buoyancy as well as in pressure. Any object immersed in water is subjected to a buoyant force. This force is equal to the weight of water that the object displaces, and it always tends to float the object. The apparent weight of the object is its actual weight minus the buoyant force. If the average density of the object is greater than the density of the water, it will float. Most objects either float or sink. However, if the density of the object is exactly equal to the density of the water, it will simply hover in space, neither floating nor sinking. But this is rare. Objects that float are positively buoyant, ones that sink are negatively buoyant, and ones that neither float nor sink are neutrally buoyant.

Shaney Frey hovers in liquid space with the aid of buoyancy. This picture was taken inside a cave, using only the light that shone down from a hole in its ceiling.

Photo by Hank Frey

Salt water weighs approximately 64 pounds per cubic foot and fresh water weighs about 62½ pounds per cubic foot. Therefore you need a little more lead weight in salt water than in fresh water to achieve nearly neutral buoyancy. An object that is neutrally buoyant in salt water will sink in fresh water.

Temperature

Depending on where you dive, the water temperature can be in the high 80s or it can be a very cold 28° Fahrenheit. Among the outstanding characteristics of water is its ability to conduct and to store heat. The thermal conductivity of water is about 25 times that of air. Except for ammonia, water has greater heat capacity—or ability to store heat—than any other liquid. These two characteristics result in a fairly rapid loss of body heat in water. Body heat loss can be reduced but not eliminated by the insulation of wet suits or by the insulation of underwear worn under dry suits. The wet suit is by far the most popular type used in recreational diving.

Hands and feet chill in water more rapidly than the rest of the body. As your hands chill, your finger dexterity and the ability to perform tasks with your hands diminishes. Cold water can cause you to loose more than half of your grip strength, making it extremely difficult for you to raise yourself out of the water. Severe chilling can even make you loose mental contact with your surroundings. It is wise to leave the water before you begin to shiver. Shivering is the body's attempt to produce more heat to offset the loss of heat to the water.

Most bodies of water do not have uniform

Cold water is a formidable adversary. Captain Ed Beckman, Medical Corps, U.S. Navy, is shown test-diving the Uniroyal electrically heated suit. Silver zinc batteries, worn around his waist, supply power. Hank Frey was the principal developer of this suit for the U.S. Navy's SeaLab II project.

Photo by Hank Frey

temperature. Instead, there is usually a layer of well-mixed warm water near the surface, a temperature transition layer (or thermocline) beneath it, then a layer that gradually gets colder toward the bottom. The top layer of water is well mixed because of surface waves. The thermocline can be very sharp, so sharp that you can actually feel it with your fingertips.

Particles tend to get trapped in the thermocline because the sharp temperature change there also gives rise to a sharp density change. A particle that is neutrally buoyant in the middle of the thermocline tends to stay there because it will be negatively buoyant if it rises a little and positively buoyant if it sinks a little. Negative buoyancy will return it to its original position if it has risen and positive buoyancy will return it to its original position if it has sunk. Such particles suspended in water reduce the light and affect the visibility.

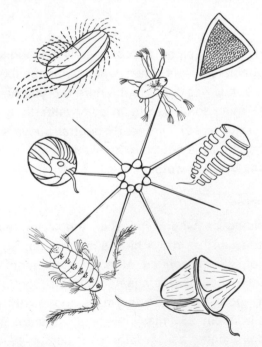

Various species of plankton. In Greek, "plankton" means "wanderer." The name is appropriate because the animals are moved helplessly with the ocean currents.

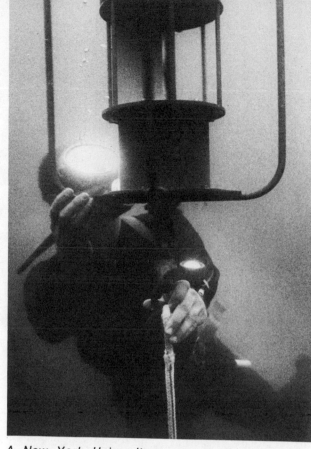

A New York University oceanographic technician examines a current meter off the coast of New Jersey. Visibility in this area ranges from a few feet to more than 50 feet depending on the presence of plankton and other particles.

Photo by Hank Frey

Objects appear one-third larger than they actually are because light rays are bent as they pass through your mask.

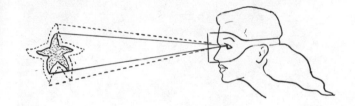

Light

The intensity of light diminishes rapidly under water. The reduced light and varying degrees of turbidity have a marked effect on visibility. Visibility ranges from less than a foot in New York harbor to more than 200 feet (under ideal conditions) in the Caribbean. Reduced visibility makes it imperative that you remain close to your buddy so that you will not lose sight of one another.

Among the most startling discoveries in store for new divers is the apparent magnification under water. Objects appear one-third larger than they actually are because light rays are bent—or refracted—as they pass from water to air. Your eye interprets the rays as having come from the direction in which they arrive. It takes some time to get used to this. Most new divers grasp at things that are just a little too far away to reach.

The various color components of light are reduced at different rates under water. The reduction of light takes place in two processes: scattering and absorption. Both of these processes involve the water molecules themselves in addition to particles—organic and inorganic—suspended in the water. Scattering causes a beam of light to be redirected in all directions. Thus, some of the energy in the beam is diverted sideways, some is diverted upward toward the surface, and the remainder penetrates deeper into the water. In addition to scattering, some of the light energy is reduced as the water molecules and suspended particles absorb light energy.

Red is reduced at a much greater rate than the other color components of light, a phenomenon that contributes to the color cast of the

The late-day sun results in long shadows on underwater scenes.

Photo by Shaney Frey

Shaney Frey's reflections from the surface are due to total internal reflection of light rays. Internal reflection occurs when you view the surface at angles from horizontal to about 40 degrees below the surface.

Photo by Hank Frey

water. Underwater scenes appear bluish in subtropical water and blue-green to yellow-green farther north. The shift from blue to yellow-green is due, in part, to dissolved yellow organic substances in the northern waters.

As you dive deeper and deeper, more and more of the red light disappears. Finally, even the most vividly colored object will appear monochromatic. This phenomenon is particularly important in underwater photography, but it influences your ability to distinguish between objects at all times.

Sound

Sound travels farther and faster under water than it does in air and is far less severely affected than light. However, your ear mechanism is not equipped to hear sounds well under water. Most of the sound energy is simply reflected from your eardrum. You will be able to hear only very intense sounds or sounds that are produced quite close to you. Even then, you may not be able to tell where the sounds come from. The location of sound depends on the slight time delay between the instant the sound reaches one ear and the instant it reaches the other one. Because the speed of sound in water is greater than it is in air, this time delay is reduced significantly and you lose your ability to tell direction.

Drag

Water opposes your movements with a force called drag. Drag is caused by the internal friction—or viscosity—of water and by the fact you must move water aside as you swim. Water has inertia as does any mass of substance, and moving water aside requires work.

Drag increases very rapidly with speed, and the energy required to maintain swimming speed increases even more rapidly. For example, to

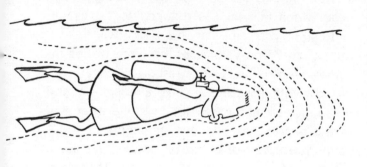

Water opposes your movements with a force called drag.

double your speed you have to exert about eight times as much energy. Swimming at a slow, rhythmic pace will conserve your energy.

The Prevention of Accidents

The one cardinal rule to follow to avoid accidents is to know your own limitations and to limit your activities accordingly. Skin and scuba diving can range from lazily snorkeling and exploring shallow reefs in warm water to combating swift currents in cold, dark, deep water. You ought to be a good judge of what activities you are capable of undertaking within the bounds of safety.

Underwater swimming can be one of the most strenuous exercises you will ever engage in. Obviously, you will have to be in excellent physical condition to do anything more than skin dive in warm, shallow water. If you are out of condition but otherwise healthy, exercise until you are ready for diving.

There are physical and psychological factors that must be considered before you decide that scuba diving is a likely pastime for you. Conditions that immediately rule out diving are: cardiovascular and respiratory diseases, perforated eardrums, and the inability to equalize pressure in the middle-ear spaces and sinuses. *Temporary* middle-ear, Eustachian tube, or sinus diseases may prevent equalization of pressure. Wait until you are well before you give it a try.

Other diseases that make diving unsafe are organic nerve disorders, epilepsy, and loss of consciousness for any reason. Nervous and emotionally unstable people as well as those who suffer from claustrophobia or vertigo tend to panic. This makes them a potential hazard to themselves and to their diving companions.

"Clearing" Your Ears

You probably have already experienced imbalanced pressure on your eardrums in an airplane or under water. The sensation is one of discomfort and it can become painful if the pressure imbalance becomes excessive. Hydrostatic pressure increases fairly rapidly under water and presses inward against your eardrums. This pressure must be balanced by the pressure inside your ears. The extreme result of imbalanced pressure is ruptured eardrums.

Pressure equalization—whether you are skin diving or scuba diving—is accomplished by forcing air into your middle-ear space via the Eustachian tubes. In diving jargon, this is called clearing your ears. There are numerous ways to do this and you will have to do a little experimenting to see which one suits you best. Many

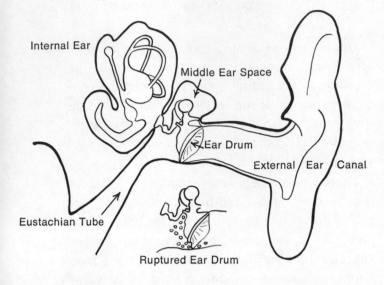

Internal Ear

Middle Ear Space

Ear Drum

External Ear Canal

Eustachian Tube

Ruptured Ear Drum

The ear.

masks have devices to help you to equalize. If you use a simple mask, you can try swallowing; pressing the bottom of the mask against your nose and blowing against closed nostrils; pressing the faceplate and blowing gently into the mask; or wearing a nose clip. Masks with nose-pinching devices make it fairly easy to clear your ears. You simply clamp your nostrils closed with your thumb and first finger and blow against the closed nostrils. You may find that a combination of methods is best. For example, swallowing in addition to blowing against closed nostrils.

A common cold or sinusitis causes congestion of mucous membranes. This congestion makes it nearly impossible to clear your ears. Therefore, you must wait until the congestion has subsided. It is best to begin clearing your ears just as soon as your head is under water. Gradual clearing as you descend is simpler than waiting until the pressure becomes uncomfortable. If you have difficulty in clearing your ears, go up a few feet and try again. If you still cannot clear, wait for a minute and try again. Never force yourself to descend if you cannot clear your ears.

Lung Squeeze

The rare accident of lung squeeze, which occurs only in skin diving among those who try to set new depth records, is just what the name implies. The lungs become compressed to less than their smallest normal volume—called residual volume. When this happens, the air sacs and tissues of the lungs become damaged and blood is forced into the lungs.

The depth limit for skin diving is determined by the ratio of the lung capacity to the residual volume. The total lung capacity is the residual volume plus the tidal volume—or the volume of the deepest breath you can take. This ratio is 4:1 for the average person. Lung squeeze can occur when this ratio is reduced to 1:1 by the hydrostatic pressure. At what depth will the 1:1 ratio occur? The volume of the lungs varies inversely with the absolute pressure. At sea level, the absolute pressure is one atmosphere and the lungs can attain their total volume when you take a deep breath. At four atmospheres of absolute pressure—or about 100 feet—the volume will be reduced by a factor of four. Therefore,

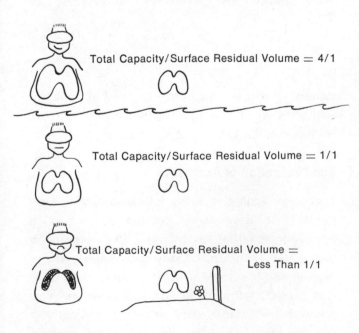

Total Capacity/Surface Residual Volume = 4/1

Total Capacity/Surface Residual Volume = 1/1

Total Capacity/Surface Residual Volume = Less Than 1/1

The mechanics of lung squeeze.

for the average person, 100 feet is the skin diving depth limit. There are many exceptions to this. During 1968, a Navy diver with an extraordinary total lung capacity to residual volume ratio dived to 217 feet. But even 100 feet is a long way down for skin diving. Limiting yourself to 20 feet for the first year of diving is a good idea. Even after years of experience, skin divers in excellent physical condition should not venture much more than 50 feet deep.

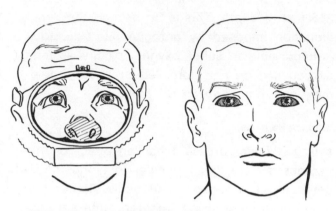

Mask squeeze and its results.

Mask Squeeze

Mask squeeze occurs during descent when the air pressure within a mask is less than that of the surrounding water. The lower pressure inside the mask acts as suction on the eyes and skin. Ruptured capillaries and vessels occur when the pressure difference increases. To avoid this, exhale into the mask through your nose as you feel the mask press against your face.

Blackout

Blackout is a more probable danger than lung squeeze. It too is a skin diving accident. And it has happened mostly among experienced divers who were determined to stay just a little longer at depth. Blackout is caused by a combination of carbon dioxide excess and insufficient oxygen.

The respiratory center of your brain controls your breathing rate to keep the partial pressure of carbon dioxide in your circulatory system at a safe level. Your respiratory center normally increases your breathing rate if there is an excess of carbon dioxide. In addition to the carbon dioxide monitoring, tiny receptors in your arteries monitor the partial pressure of oxygen and transmit this information to your respiratory center. The respiratory center reacts to increase your breathing whenever the partial pressure of oxygen approaches a critical value.

The urge to breathe when you hold your breath is due to the increase of carbon dioxide. This is usually a strong urge but with stubbornness, you can ignore it and continue to hold your breath. If you do this, more oxygen will be converted to carbon dioxide until the partial pressure of oxygen in your lungs approaches the critical level required to sustain life. You may or may not feel a weaker second warning to expel the air in your lungs and to ventilate them with fresh air.

If you overstay yourself at any depth, you can easily encounter blackout. How does this work? Suppose you decide to head for the surface just at the moment when you have reached the critical partial pressure of oxygen. As you ascend, the pressure around you decreases, and, accordingly, the partial pressure of the oxygen in your lungs also decreases. This additional lowering of the oxygen partial pressure causes severe lack of oxygen and loss of consciousness. Divers who get into this predicament rarely reach the surface. They either drown or are pulled out of the water weak and subdued. Many of these victims are negatively loaded with excess lead and sink when they lose consciousness.

If you are dissatisfied with the depth and length of your snorkel dives, use scuba. The risks involved in extending underwater time while skin diving are too dangerous.

Overexertion

Any task is much more difficult to perform under water than it is above the surface. You will have to guard against overexerting yourself because this can lead to unconsciousness. And unconsciousness can lead to drowning. The initial symptom is the feeling that you are out of breath. Stop whatever you are doing and catch your breath. Overexertion does not usually occur if you are doing a simple task or when you are swimming at a reasonable speed—unless you are battling a strong current. However, it may happen if you work feverishly to perform some heavy task and become so involved in the task that you ignore your own safety. Insufficient sleep and some degree of motion sickness will accelerate the onset of overexertion.

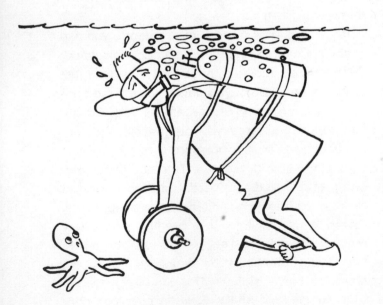

Don't overexert yourself!

Oxygen Toxicity

Oxygen, the one gas required to support life, becomes severely toxic at elevated pressures. It becomes toxic to most people in a short time when the partial pressure exceeds about two atmospheres absolute. This corresponds to breathing pure oxygen at about 33 feet deep. Some people cannot tolerate even this pressure of oxygen. *Rebreathers use pure oxygen and are extremely dangerous.* They should be used only by trained, military underwater swimmers. The partial pressure of oxygen in compressed air becomes two atmospheres absolute at about 315 feet of depth. This is far beyond the depth limitation imposed by nitrogen narcosis, so it is impossible to suffer oxygen toxicity as long as you use only compressed-air scuba equipment and remain above 130 feet.

Nitrogen Narcosis

Nitrogen under pressure has an effect on the nervous system that is similar to being intoxicated. It does not happen suddenly. Rather, it is a sort of drunkenness by degree. Different people react to it in different ways but, for everyone, nitrogen narcosis means impaired judgment and a marked decrease in the ability to perform tasks. It is not a permanent or traumatic condition in itself. However, it can easily trigger accidents.

Most people are affected by nitrogen narcosis by the time they reach 100 feet. At depths much greater than 130 feet, the symptoms become very noticeable. It is for this reason that 130 feet is a reasonable limiting depth for compressed-air scuba.

Air Embolism

If any diving accident had to be singled out as the most dreadful, it would be air embolism. The mortality rate for those who suffer from air em-

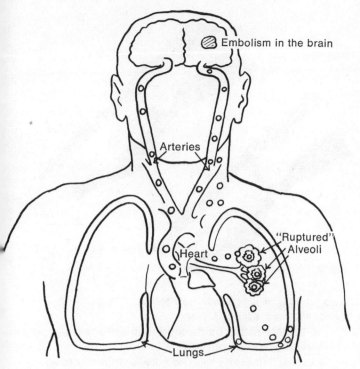

The mechanics of air embolism. (Only one lung is shown overexpanded for the sake of illustration.)

bolism is higher than 90 percent. Air embolism occurs when the lungs overexpand to the point that air bubbles are forced through the air sacs of the lungs into the circulatory system. The bubbles can become lodged in the heart, the arteries, or the brain.

Overexpansion of the lungs is the result of holding your breath when you ascend. Recall that the volume of a compressible object increases as the depth decreases. If you take a deep breath at 33 feet, hold your breath, and rise to the surface, your lungs would be twice the size—if they did not burst on the way. But they would. *Always breathe normally while ascending with scuba.* Never hold your breath when you ascend. This simple rule will assure you of avoiding air embolism and related accidents.

The symptoms of air embolism appear within minutes—even seconds—after surfacing. In cases where divers hold their breath from deep water, the symptoms may appear even before they reach the surface. Unconsciousness sometimes precedes the symptoms. Air embolism usually attacks mental processes initially. Dizziness, confusion, weakness, and blurred vision are followed by more severe symptoms: collapse and unconsciousness. Convulsions and death may follow. A bloody froth may or may not appear in the victim's mouth. Not all the symptoms of air embolism may be present in a particular case. Do not assume that it is not air embolism if, for instance, you do not see the bloody froth.

Accidents very closely related to air embolism include pneumothorax, mediastinal emphysema, and subcutaneous emphysema. They are all caused by overexpansion of the lungs.

Pneumothorax is a pocket of air formed inside the chest cavity but it is formed outside of the lungs. An expanding pneumothorax can collapse the lungs and push the heart to one side. Difficulty in breathing accompanied by a sharp pain in the chest are the usual symptoms.

Mediastinal emphysema is the formation of air in the tissues of the mediastinum, or middle of the chest. Its symptoms include difficulty in breathing, shock, and blueness of the skin, lips, or fingernails.

Air embolism and related accidents are much more likely to occur near the surface, where the volume changes are more rapid than at greater depths. Most accidents involving overexpansion of the lungs occur because of panic. You must always keep a cool head and guard against panicking. If you are ever forced to ascend because your breathing apparatus is nonfunctional, exhale all the way to the surface. The hydrostatic pressure will not force air out of your lungs; you must do it yourself.

Carbon Dioxide and Carbon Monoxide

Carbon dioxide excess is not a problem so long as you use commercially available scuba equipment and remain above 130 feet. It is possible for carbon dioxide to build up in the so-called dead-air spaces in breathing apparatus, but modern equipment for sport divers does not have this deficiency.

Excess carbon dioxide can also be caused by skip-breathing—or holding your breath for short intervals—with scuba. The symptoms are rapid deep breathing, headache, and dizziness. It can lead to unconsciousness, which can in turn lead to drowning.

Carbon monoxide excess is usually the result of a poorly designed or poorly operated air station. Exhaust fumes from a gasoline-driven compressor are responsible for the presence of carbon monoxide in compressed air. Compressors using oil-lubrication sometimes "diesel"—or ignite the oil—contributing carbon monoxide to the compressed air. If you use a portable, gasoline-driven compressor, always place the exhaust downwind of the intake. Many states require inspection of commercial air stations, and even in states where there is no such requirement, dive-shop owners are usually quite careful about the quality of their compressed air.

The dangerous aspect of carbon monoxide poisoning is the lack of sufficient warning: you can lose consciousness before realizing anything is amiss. Any degree of carbon monoxide poisoning requires prompt medical attention. Brain damage is inevitable if a victim becomes comatose. Pure oxygen under pressure is the usual treatment—not to exceed 20 pounds per square inch for more than 90 minutes. If this is not available, pure oxygen at one atmosphere of pressure is acceptable and mandatory.

The Bends

The bends—alias decompression sickness, alias caisson disease—is caused by the formation of nitrogen bubbles during ascent after a fairly prolonged and deep dive. The nitrogen in compressed air is absorbed by the fluids and tissues in your body when you are subjected to pressure. The pressure is reduced as you ascend, and the nitrogen is then released from the fluids and tissues, passes through your veins, and leaves your body via the lungs. If you do not exceed

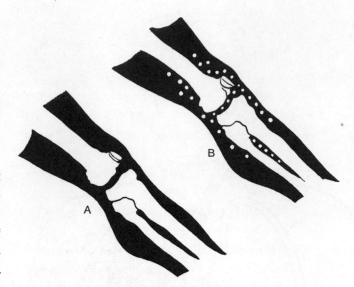

Decompression sickness, commonly called the bends suffered at the knee.
(a) Leg tissues (black) saturated with nitrogen after a prolonged deep dive.
(b) Nitrogen bubbles form and become entrapped around the knee when ascent is too rapid.

the no-decompression limits of the standard air decompression table, and if you ascend no faster than 60 feet per minute, this is what normally occurs. However, if you do not take these precautions, bubbles of nitrogen will form because the gas just cannot be removed quickly enough by your bloodstream. The blood is able to carry only limited amounts of nitrogen away.

The degree of injury depends on the size of the bubbles and where they become lodged. If bubbles form in the brain, lungs, or spinal cord, decompression sickness can be fatal. In any other part of the body, the bubbles can cause great discomfort that develops into unbearable pain. The symptoms range from itchy skin to stiff joints, partial or total paralysis, blindness, and convulsions.

If you do not exceed the time-depth combination shown in Table 1, decompression will not be required. It is wise to avoid decompression if at all possible because decompression tables are not foolproof. A small percentage of incidents is expected by the Navy, but they have recompression chambers on hand for immediate treatment. The limited supply of air in a scuba tank makes decompression risky business. If you run out of air before you complete decompressing, you undoubtedly will suffer the bends.

Bottom time is the time spent descending plus the actual time on the bottom—or at the depth. To assure yourself of safe diving, use the next deepest depth and the next longest bottom time if you should ever have to decompress.

It is suggested that you study the U.S. Navy's decompression tables and the instructions for their use reproduced in Appendix C. The tables include repetitive dives as well as single dives.

Table 1. Bottom Time Limits for No Decompression*

Depth (feet)	Bottom Time (minutes)
30 (or less)	no limit
35	310 (5 hours, 10 minutes)
40	200 (3 hours, 20 minutes)
50	100 (1 hour, 40 minutes)
60	60 (1 hour)
70	50
80	40
90	30
100	25
110	20
120	15
130	10
Deeper—unsafe for recreational diving.	

*This table is based on ascending at the rate of 60 feet per minute.

Rescue Methods

The first rule of self-rescue is to remain calm—otherwise you cannot do yourself a bit of good. Evaluate a bad underwater situation quickly and decide what you have to do. If you are skin diving or if your scuba air supply is nil, time is especially important. Appendix A lists the most common accidents, their symptoms and treatment.

Free yourself of obstacles by maneuvering your body or by cutting entanglements with your knife. Drop your weight belt and head for the surface. Remember to breathe normally with functioning scuba or to exhale all the way up when making a free ascent.

Inflate your safety float and cling to your diver's float. Try not to take deep, gasping breaths or you may hyperventilate until you are weak and dizzy. You need not remove your scuba unless it is particularly bothersome. Rest until you have regained your strength.

Diving rescues may vary from sharing air to towing an unconscious victim to shore. Your first duty is to keep yourself out of danger. If you don't, you will be useless to the victim and to yourself.

Get an underwater victim to the surface—the regulator is a convenient towing handle. If he isn't breathing, try to force the compressed air out of his lungs by wrapping your legs around his stomach and squeezing. This will elevate his diaphragm and force the air out. If no air comes out, he probably exhaled it on his last breath. Release his weights and inflate his safety float to help raise him. On the surface, start mouth-to-mouth resuscitation immediately. If he is unconscious but breathing, don't begin artificial respiration. Keep his head out of the water and tow him to safety, using your diver's float to support him. Be sure to inflate your own safety float. Because he lost consciousness underwater, you must assume that he needs recompression.

A struggling, conscious victim is dangerous to you. Do not make contact with him. Be ready to swim away rapidly if he lunges for you. Even your best friend will try to climb up on you in order to get air. Talk to him and try to assure him that you can get him in safely if he doesn't struggle. Urge him to inflate his safety float and drop his weights. Offer him something to hold on to. Extend your diver's float, *unloaded* speargun, camera housing, or even snorkel.

A scuba tank is slightly buoyant when its air supply is depleted, but even so, it is cumbersome and causes water drag. You may find it easier to help him into shore if his tank is off.

If you learn at least two of the many methods

of artificial respiration, you should be able to cope with any situation. Mouth-to-mouth is by far the most effective way to move air in and out of a victim's lungs. Back pressure—arm lift is a good alternative.

Before you give any kind of artificial respiration, quickly loosen any clothing around the neck, get the victim into position, and clear his mouth with your fingers. Be careful not to push anything farther down his throat. Make sure his throat is clear and open. Get into your position and start immediately. Time is vitally important. Do this yourself only if you are alone. Continue giving artificial respiration at the rate of 10 to 12 cycles per minute without interruption. Get others to tend to first aid and to seek medical assistance.

Apply artificial respiration for at least four hours or until a physician has pronounced the victim dead. As soon as breathing resumes, stop.

Mouth-to-mouth resuscitation can be started immediately, while you are still in the water. Support the victim on a diver's float. Clear his mouth. Hold his jaw in a "jutting-out" position with one hand and close his nostrils with the other. Tilt his head back. Take a deep breath, and form a seal with your lips over his mouth.

Breathe into him slowly and steadily until his chest expands. If he doesn't inflate easily, his airways may be blocked. Quickly recheck his throat. After you inflate him, remove your mouth, inhale, allow him to exhale, and repeat the cycle. If he doesn't exhale, squeeze his chest gently.

S-shaped plastic tubes are available for mouth-to-mouth insufflation. Inflation is easier, but you take the risk of damaging the victim's throat tissues. Also, you should not have to depend on plastic airways or any other piece of equipment. However, you can cut your snorkel at the center of its curvature and use it as a breathing tube.

An alternative method is the back pressure—

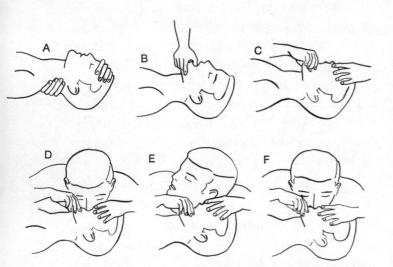

Mouth-to-mouth artificial respiration.
(a) Tilt the victim's head back so that the chin points upward.
(b) Pull or push the jaw into a jutting-out position to open the airway.
(c) Hold the mouth open and pinch the nostrils shut.
(d) Open your mouth wide, place it tightly over the victim's mouth and blow.
(e) Turn your head to the side; listen for victim's exhalation as you take another breath.
(f) Repeat blowing effort.

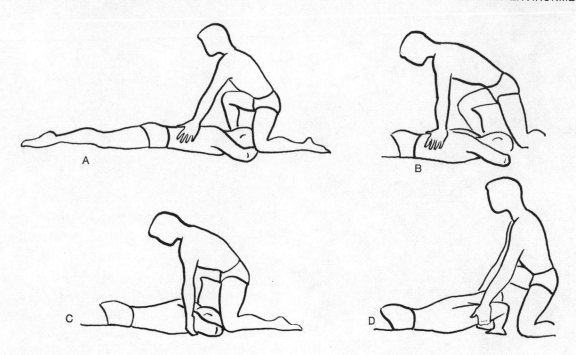

Back pressure–arm lift artificial respiration.
(a) Starting position.
(b) Rock forward and press slowly and steadily.

(c) Grasp arms just above elbows and rock back-
    ward.
(d) Raise arms as you continue to rock backward.

arm lift technique. Check the mouth and throat
for obstacles. Kneel at the victim's head and
place your hands on his back, just below the
shoulder blades. Your thumbs should point
toward each other with their tips barely touching. Rock forward and press gently until your
shoulders are directly above your hands. The
pressing action should be smooth and steady.
Release the pressure and start rocking backward. Move your hands along the victim's sides
and grasp his arms above his elbows. Continue
rocking backward naturally. Pull his arms
toward you until you feel the resistance of his
shoulder blades. Then lower his arms and repeat the cycle. The keynote is rhythm.

Do not press too hard or you may injure his
ribs. Do not use this method if the victim has a
chest injury. Use mouth-to-mouth instead.

Coauthor Shaney Frey collects limestone samples in
a Florida cave. Scuba diving permits you to go
deeper and to stay longer than skin diving.
Photo by Hank Frey

4 | Scuba Diving Equipment

Scuba diving gives you greater freedom and more time to explore under water than skin diving. You can safely go deeper and stay longer if you apply the cautions in the preceding chapter.

The equipment to be added to your basic skin diving equipment is more complex and more expensive. You can purchase and maintain scuba equipment more intelligently if you learn about the principles of its operation. It is not necessary for you to know the function of every nut and bolt, but a general knowledge will be enough for you to know when your equipment needs attention. It is a good idea to buy your equipment from a dive shop that repairs equipment in addition to selling it.

For scuba diving, you need the following equipment: a compressed-air tank with a valve and a back pack (or harness), a demand regulator, a weight belt (or additional weights if you already own a belt), a depth gauge, and a watch (if you dive deeper than 30 feet). Optional accessories include a tank-pressure gauge (both surface and underwater types), a light, a compass, a lift bag, an underwater slate, and a decompression meter.

Tanks

Tanks for scuba diving are usually made of chrome-molybdenum steel. The outside surface is galvanized, and the deluxe models are coated with vinyl in various colors including white, black, orange, and yellow. The inside of scuba tanks are subjected to corrosion due to moisture in compressed air, but good ones are internally protected by nontoxic coatings that minimize rust and corrosion.

Some tanks are buoyant when they are empty, others, nonbuoyant. Buoyant tanks—or neutrally buoyant tanks—are preferable because they are a little easier to handle and a little easier to swim with.

The Interstate Commerce Commission (ICC) is the agency responsible for governing all high-pressure tanks in the United States except those used by the military services. Compressed-air tanks for scuba diving are marked according to ICC regulations and must pass ICC tests every five years. The markings on scuba tanks include the serial number (registered with the U.S. Bureau of Mines), the pressure rating, the manufacturer, and the date of manufacture. The pressure rating is prefixed either by ICC3A or by ICC3AA. The most common pressure rating for scuba tanks is 2,250 pounds per square inch. The range is from 1,800 psi to 2,600 psi when the tank is at 70° Fahrenheit.

The operators of compressed-air stations are permitted to fill your tanks only if the tanks are properly marked and have been inspected within the past five years. The law allows them to fill tanks to 10 percent over the marked pressure rating if the rating is followed by a plus sign

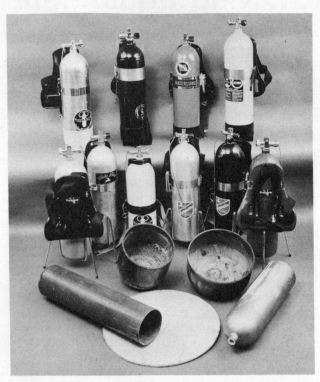

A variety of scuba tanks, including partially completed ones in the foreground.

Courtesy Skin Diver Magazine

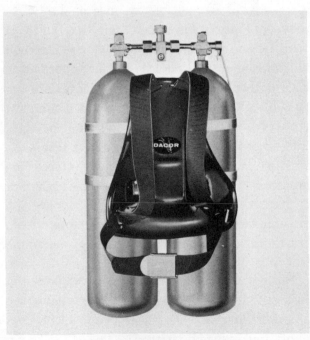

A set of double tanks with a reserve valve and harness.

Courtesy Dacor Corporation

and if the tank is fitted with an approved safety device. For example, a tank marked ICC3A—2,250+ and fitted with a safety device can be filled to 2,475 psi. Tanks become warm while they are being filled, and the increased temperature makes them expand. For this reason, well-run air stations put the tanks in a large drum of water to keep them from overheating during filling.

Tanks also undergo an increase in pressure if they are subjected to the heat of strong sunlight. White tanks and galvanized tanks absorb less light energy—less heat—than black or colored ones. Regardless of the outside finish on your tank, keep it in the shade rather than in the direct sunlight. Cover it with a blanket if there is no shaded area.

The standard tank for scuba diving is called a 72; it has a nominal capacity of 72 cubic feet of air. The actual capacity is 71.2 cubic feet of air at atmospheric pressure. The inside volume of the tank is less than one-half cubic foot. Among the other tank capacities are the 38 and the 53. The 53s are about 20 percent lighter than 72s, which makes them more comfortable for female divers.

Valves

Scuba tanks are equipped with valves for two reasons: they are used to turn on and to turn off the flow of air from the tank, and they are used as a place for clamping the regulator. There are valves for single tanks and valves for double tanks. There are essentially two different types of valves, called K valves and J valves.

The K valve is simply an on-off valve, and the J valve is designed to let you know when your tank is nearly depleted of air. K valves are less expensive than J valves, and after you have accumulated some time with scuba, they are all right with just a few reservations. You must never enter a cave or a wreck when you use a K valve because they give you very little notice that you

The standard tank for scuba diving has a nominal capacity of 72 cubic feet of free air at atmospheric pressure.

Photo by Paul Tzimoulis, Skin Diver Magazine

are running out of air. It just becomes more and more difficult to breathe and you must ascend immediately to make breathing easier.

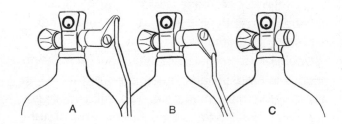

Tank valves.
(a) Reserve valve (J) in diving position.
(b) Reserve valve (J) in reserve position.
(c) K valve.

The J valve is designed so that your air supply is cut off when you have 300 psi remaining in your single tank or when you have 500 psi remaining in one of your double tanks. You must then manually reset the valve to obtain the reserve air supply. This type of valve, properly used, is the most foolproof one. Some J valves let you know by a sonic signal when you are approaching your reserve air. You can either buy your tanks with J valves and use any regulator or buy your tanks with K valves and use a regulator with a built-in J valve. A regulator with a built-in J valve will save you money if you buy more than one tank.

The lever of the spring-loaded J valve must be in the up position if it is to give you proper warning. You pull down on a pull rod to release the reserve air. The lever is left in the down position until after your tank has been refilled. J valves are sometimes accidentally moved downward during a dive. Check your valve from time to time to be sure it is in the up position. If it has been moved, push it back up. You will still have reserve air providing that your tank pressure exceeds 300 psi (500 psi for doubles).

Back Packs

Back packs are available both for single tanks and for double tank assemblies. Some packs are designed for both. The most modern back packs are contoured to the back and hips, are made of high-impact plastics and stainless steel, permit quick and easy removal and replacement of tanks, have an adjustable nylon harness, and are equipped with a corrosion-resistant quick-release buckle.

Harnesses are less expensive than back packs. Although they are not as convenient as the more elaborate back packs, harnesses can serve the purpose quite well.

One of a wide variety of back packs for scuba tanks. Courtesy Voit Rubber Company

Regulators

The purpose of a regulator is to supply you with air as you require it and at the proper pressure. Regulators are designed to reduce the pressure of the air in your scuba tank so that the air you breathe is at the same pressure as the surrounding water. They are also designed to deliver air to you upon demand—only when you inhale. For this reason, they are known as demand regulators.

The most important thing to look for in a regulator is easy breathing. There is a false notion that a regulator that is hard to breathe from will increase the duration of your air supply. This is not true. A hard breathing regulator will cause fatigue and, if anything, will also cause you to use your air supply more rapidly. Ask your dive shop to recommend a regulator that provides constant easy breathing throughout the entire duration of your dive. Some regulators are easy to breathe from at the beginning of a dive but get more difficult toward the end of a dive. Breathing is more difficult at the beginning of a dive and easier toward the end with others. A well-designed regulator makes it easy to breathe from the beginning to the end of a dive.

There are two ways to categorize regulators. First, there are single-hose and double-hose regulators. Then, there are one-stage and two-stage regulators. The one-stage regulator reduces the high-pressure air in just one stage, but the two-stage regulator accomplishes this in two stages —or steps. The one-stage regulator is available only in the double-hose design. The most popular ones currently in use are in the single-hose, two-stage category.

Double-hose regulators have one inhalation hose and one exhaust hose. Nonreturn valves are situated in the mouthpiece so that water cannot enter the inhalation hose from the mouthpiece or the mouthpiece from the exhalation hose. These valves resemble flat mushrooms. All the mechanical parts of the regulator are

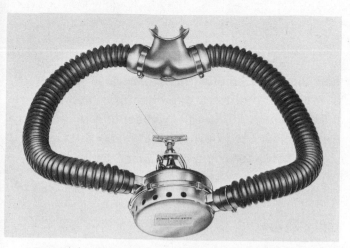

Double-hose regulators have one inhalation hose and one exhalation hose. The pressure-reducing mechanisms are together in one housing. There are two types: one-stage pressure reduction and two-stage pressure reduction.

Courtesy U.S. Divers Company

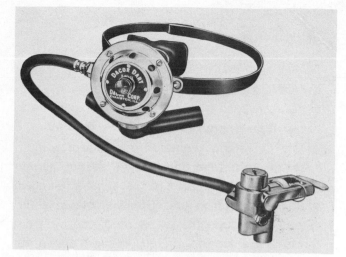

The single-hose regulator reduces tank pressure in two stages. One stage is mounted on the tank valve, and the second stage is incorporated into the mouthpiece assembly.

Courtesy Dacor Corporation

housed in one assembly, which is clamped to the valve on your scuba tank. Part of the housing is flooded with water while the other part, containing the pressure-reducing mechanisms, is filled with air. The two parts are separated by a large diaphragm, which senses any difference between the water pressure and the air pressure.

The one-stage regulator employs a series of levers activated by the diaphragm. When you take a breath, the diaphragm is deflected inward by the water pressure. This deflection activates the levers to open a valve, permitting more air to flow from the tank. The ease of breathing with a one-stage regulator varies with the pressure in the scuba tank. Also, the initial force required

The single-hose regulator has become the more popular type. This lovely lass has made a good choice of equipment: single-hose regulator, reserve valve on a single tank, and a comfortable back pack.

Photo by Paul Zimoulkis, Skin Diver Magazine

to activate the mechanism is slightly greater than it is with two-stage models. One-stage regulators are less reliable and more expensive to repair than single-hose, two-stage regulators.

The two-stage regulator consists of a high-pressure first stage and a low-pressure second stage. Both are located in the same housing in double-hose regulators. The first stage is designed to reduce the pressure of the air from the tank pressure to a fixed pressure above the water pressure. This fixed pressure is usually about 100 psi above the water pressure. Air equal in pressure to the surrounding water is delivered to you from the second stage as you demand it.

The mouthpiece of a double-hose regulator can be cleared of water by holding it higher than the regulator housing. This causes a free flow of air. Or it can be cleared by exhaling into it.

All single-hose regulators employ two stages: the first stage is in a separate housing clamped to the tank valve; the second stage is in a housing that also contains the mouthpiece. A single, medium-pressure intake hose connects them. There is no need for a separate exhaust hose because the second stage housing is equipped with air outlets designed so that the bubbles will not be released directly in front of your face.

The first and second stages of the single-hose regulator perform the same functions as they do in the double-hose regulator although they are designed a little differently.

The mouthpiece of a single-hose regulator is cleared by pressing a button, which deflects the pressure-sensing diaphragm.

Weight Belt

If you do not already own a weight belt, see Chapter One for the requirements of a good weight belt. You need more weight for scuba diving than you do for skin diving. The exact amount will depend on what kind of tank, back pack, and regulator you buy. A standard tank weighs about 5 pounds more when it is filled than when it is empty. This means that you will be more buoyant toward the end of a dive than at the beginning. To partially offset this variation in buoyancy, put a few extra pounds of weight on your belt after you have trimmed your weight for the scuba equipment.

Depth Gauge

A depth gauge is part of your defense against the bends if you dive deeper than 30 feet. It lets you know, within various accuracies, how deep you are. This is one of two things you must know to compute how long you can stay at that depth without the need for decompression. The other is time.

Depth gauges work on several different principles. The gauge that gives the most accurate readings is the oil-filled type. Look for a gauge that reads about 130 feet at full scale. This is as deep as you ought to go. The shallow-depth readings will be more accurate with a gauge that

Depth gauge.

Courtesy U.S. Divers Company

reads to 130 feet (or 150 feet) than one that reads to greater depths. If you ever have to use your depth gauge for decompression, you will need to have the best accuracy possible for the 10-foot stop.

Watch

If you dive deeper than 30 feet, you will need a watch. There is a tremendous assortment of watches within a wide price range to choose from. A good watch is easy to read even in very dim light, is guaranteed pressureproof and watertight to at least three times the maximum depth of your dives, has a sweep second hand, and is equipped with a movable bezel.

Diver's watches with external bezels and sweep second hands.

Courtesy Zodiac Watch Company

The bezel will help you to keep track of the time elapsed since the beginning of the dive. Some watches have external bezels; others incorporate them within the watch case. Watches with external bezels require only one crown to wind and set the watch; ones with an internal bezel require a second crown for adjusting the bezel. This is one more opening, which theoretically increases the chance of water trickling into the watch case. In practice, most two-crown watches are as reliable as one-crown watches. The internal bezel has one major advantage: it is almost impossible to move the internal bezel by accident after you have set it.

The sweep second hand is important because it can help you to monitor your rate of ascent. The decompression tables are based on an ascent rate of 60 feet per minute. This corresponds to 1 foot per second. A good way to judge your rate of ascent is to rise 5 feet (according to your depth gauge) for every 5 seconds (according to your watch). Wear your watch and your depth gauge on one wrist so you can read both at the same glance.

Your watch will be invaluable if you ever exceed the no-decompression limits and are forced to decompress.

There are other uses for a watch—above the surface. A diver's watch is a real conversation piece. Other divers will notice it and challenge you with their sea stories. They are never-failing eye catchers at a cocktail party. You will never have to baldly offer that you are a diver. You will be asked, "What kind of watch is that?" Then you can tell your repertoire of diving stories by request rather than "voluntarily."

Air Station

An air station is economically feasible only for large groups of scuba divers or, of course, for dive shops. You can find air stations even in many of the most remote diving locations.

The simplest air station is a high-pressure

High-pressure compressor.
Courtesy Skin Diver Magazine

compressor specifically designed to fill scuba tanks. Compressors are driven either by electric motors or by gasoline engines. You must guard against carbon monoxide with gasoline-driven engines by placing the compressor intake upwind of the engine exhaust. A filter, air purifier, filling gauge, and water barrel complete the set-up.

Compressors are rated in cfm (cubic feet per minute) and vary from about 1 cfm to more than 15 cfm. The weight, size, and cost of a compressor increase with increased capacity. You will have to be satisfied with a compressor that takes about an hour to fill a tank if you want portability or economy.

Commercial air-station owners generally fill large storage tanks from a compressor. Scuba tanks are filled directly from the storage tanks. When filling scuba tanks from a bank of storage tanks, you must employ a specific sequence in turning valves. Initially, the valve on each storage tank is closed. Place your tank in the water barrel and clamp the filling gauge to it. Open the valve on the scuba tank. Then, open the valve on the storage tank having the lowest pressure. Adjust the rate of flow so that the tank does not get hot. When the filling gauge needle ceases to move, the pressure in the scuba tank is the same as the pressure in the storage tank. Close the storage tank valve. Then go on to the tank with the next highest air pressure. Continue this process until you have "capped off" your tank to the highest pressure in the bank. But do not exceed the rated pressure on your scuba tank. You can exceed it by 10 percent only if the plus sign

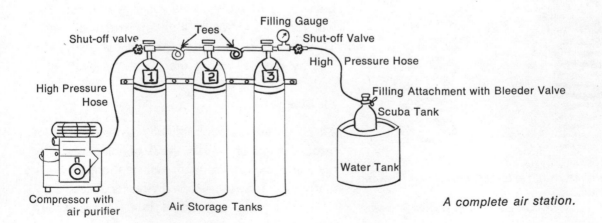

A complete air station.

appears after the rating and if the tank is equipped with a blow-off valve.

Tank-Pressure Gauge

The purpose of a tank-pressure gauge—or simply pressure gauge—is to enable you to get a measure of how much time you will have at depth. There are few things more frustrating than going through the agony of putting on all your equipment, getting to the bottom, and running out of air in the first few minutes.

There are two types of pressure gauges: those that can be used only above the surface and those that are attached to your scuba regulator by a length of high-pressure hose. The underwater type is especially useful during deep dives in which you intend to decompress. The gauge tells you, within a somewhat questionable accuracy, whether or not you will have enough air for the decompression stop. All pressure gauges suffer inaccuracies at low-pressure readings. Every group of divers should have at least one pressure gauge for checking tank pressures before and after dives.

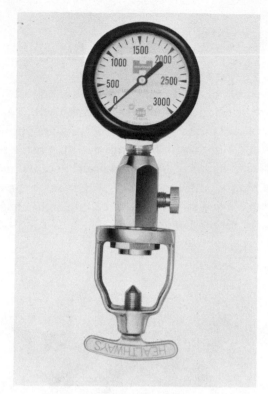

Underwater tank-pressure gauge.

A powerful and rugged diver's light.

Photo by Hank Frey

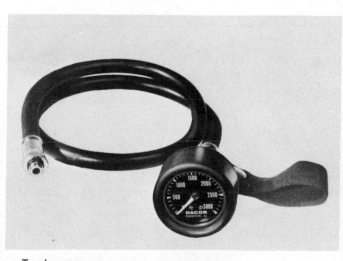

Tank-pressure gauge.

Courtesy Dacor Corporation

Light

An underwater light comes in very handy when you are looking for lobsters or when you want to see objects in more detail. The brightest portable hand light available employs 10 flashlight batteries in a sturdy aluminum housing equipped with a magnetic switch. Most of the less expensive models use lantern batteries in plastic housings with toggle switches.

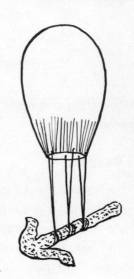

Lift bag for salvage work.

Diver's compass.

Courtesy U.S. Divers Company

Lift Bag

Lift bags are salvage devices. The simplest and most foolproof lift bag resembles a tall parachute. The shroud lines are attached to a metal ring. You lash the ring to whatever you want to lift to the surface. The bag is filled by holding your mouthpiece under it and allowing air to flow. The air will expand as the bag travels toward the surface but the expanding air will vent out

Compass

Despite the fact that you wear a magnetic steel tank while scuba diving, compasses can be used for underwater navigation. Good compasses are affected by scuba tanks only when they are less than about a foot away. Navy underwater swimmers are required to follow a complex underwater route using their compasses without surfacing to check their bearings. This can be done with adequate practice.

Plastic "slate" and grease pencil.

Having chosen the proper equipment, the next step is to learn both individual and team skills in a swimming pool under the careful eye of a qualified instructor.

Photo by Paul Tzimoulis, Skin Diver Magazine

from the open bottom. Lift bags designed for scuba diving have lifting capacities from 100 pounds to 1,000 pounds. The smallest bags require the equivalent of 2 minutes of your air supply at 33 feet of depth.

Underwater Slate

White plastic "slates" and grease pencils are used for making notes under water. It takes too long to write complex messages, so they are hardly useful for communicating with buddy divers. They are convenient for noting scientific observations, keeping track of camera exposures, and sketching small scenes.

Decompression Meter

Decompression meters are available that will program your decompression requirements regardless of the time-depth history of your dive. They compute decompression automatically for repetitive dives as well as for single dives.

Chuck Niklin, a top-flight diver and photographer, pauses to view the scenery off Los Coronodos Islands, Mexico.

Photo by Hank Frey

5 | Scuba Diving Techniques

It is possible to learn skin diving techniques on your own, and safely, but you must learn the scuba diving skills under the watchful eye of an instructor. There are at least two important reasons for this. First, it is critical that you learn all the scuba skills to the point that they become second nature and you can perform them quickly and with precision. Second, without proper guidance, you can do yourself harm even in a swimming pool when you are breathing compressed air.

There are thousand of instructors in the United States—and many abroad. You will probably have little difficulty locating one. The three major national organizations that certify instructors are NAUI (National Association of Underwater Instructors), PADI (Professional Association of Diving Instructors), and the YMCA. The Los Angeles County Department of Recreation also certifies instructors to teach in that area. Many compressed-air stations will not refill scuba tanks unless you can show a diver's certificate. Some are bound by local laws, but others follow this procedure mainly because they feel a special responsibility to the public. In addition to air stations, many charter-boat captains and diving guides require you to have a certificate.

Plan on spending a minimum of 10 hours learning the skills in a swimming pool. You will also have to allow ample time to study and to understand the principles of scuba diving, scuba equipment, and underwater physiology.

Medical Examination

All certified scuba instructors require you to have a medical examination before they will accept you as a student. There are valid reasons

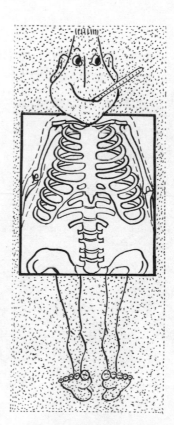

A medical examination is a must before learning to scuba dive.

for this. As a scuba diver, you will be equipped to venture far below the surface and remain there for fairly long periods of time—even without making decompression dives. For example, you can remain at 60 feet for almost an hour—and 60 feet is a long way up and an hour is a long time, especially if you are exerting yourself. To scuba dive safely, you must know your skills thoroughly, be cool witted, and be physically capable of coping with all situations. You will be unsafe not only to yourself but also to your buddy divers if you become incapacitated for any reason—physical or psychological.

Relatively few physicians are trained in submarine and diving medicine. However, there have been numerous articles about diving problems in medical journals over the past 15 years, so most doctors will at least be familiar with your examination requirements. You should take it upon yourself to offer any information you can regarding your psychological history as well as your medical history.

The following disorders rule out diving: cardiovascular and respiratory diseases, permanent inability to equalize sinus and middle-ear pressure differentials, persistent otitis or sinusitis, perforated eardrum, organic neurological disorders, history of epilepsy, and loss of consciousness for any cause. Panic occurs most frequently with people who are emotionally unstable and extremely nervous, who suffer from vertigo or claustrophobia, or who have not received thorough training.

The Buddy System

The buddy system is an absolute must for safe scuba diving. Unless you concentrate on staying

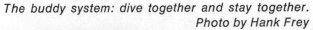

The buddy system: dive together and stay together.
Photo by Hank Frey

well within vision of one another, it is easy to become separated at depth. You should check frequently (especially in turbid water), because it takes only an instant for your buddy to disappear beyond the limit of visibility. If it becomes necessary for your buddy to surface for any reason, accompany him to the surface. Go down together, stay together, and come up together. Follow this rule and you will never become a statistic in the gruesome files of those who perished because they insisted on diving alone.

There are a number of things that can go wrong, and your buddy diver's aid may be imperative. For example, you can become almost inextricably entangled in kelp or lines when they become snarled around your tank valve and regulator. You cannot see directly behind you and it is often impossible to disentangle yourself just by feeling. Although equipment failures are extremely rare, you might have to buddy-breathe if your scuba becomes inoperative. For this reason alone, you and your buddy should never be separated by more than about 10 feet even when the visibility is unlimited.

Always dive with a buddy and stay with him; never dive alone.

Handling Equipment

Modern scuba equipment will serve you well and for many years if you handle it and maintain it properly. It takes very little extra effort to do this.

Most of the items in your diver's bag cannot be damaged by mechanical shock, but your regulator, mask, depth gauge, and tank-pressure gauge are susceptible to damage. When you pack your bag, put your weight belt in the bottom, then pack your fins, wet suit, safety vest, snorkel, gauges, and regulator and put your mask on top. Some diver's bags have pockets for small or fragile items. Carry your tank separately by cradling it in your arms or by holding it by the back pack. It is not wise to hold a tank

by its valve, especially when your hands are cold or wet—you might drop it.

Most regulators are rugged and can withstand a reasonable amount of abuse. But avoid banging your regulator against hard objects such as your tank or the deck of a boat. The second stage of a single-hose regulator, dangling from the end of the hose, is particularly susceptible to shocks. When you pick up a single-hose regulator, hold both stages in your hand. Pick up a double-hose regulator by the yoke that clamps it to the tank valve and support the mouthpiece with your other hand. This precaution will prevent moving parts from being knocked out of alignment.

All regulator manufacturers provide a plastic cap to keep dust, dirt, and liquids out of the regulator mechanism. Keep the cap in place at all times when your regulator is not mounted on your tank valve. Just before you mount the regulator, open the valve slightly for an instant to blow any foreign particles out of the valve opening (known as "cracking the valve"). Keep the valve clean by covering it with masking tape as soon as your tank has been refilled.

Always check the tank pressure before you mount the regulator onto the valve. Crack the valve and clamp your regulator handtight. You do not have to use tools because O-rings will seal with very little pressure. Then check the regulator by taking several deep breaths and listen closely for air escaping from the valve. When you remove the regulator, close the tank valve and inhale whatever air is left inside your regulator. If you do not do this, a pressure lock will form and it will be difficult to remove the regulator. You can simply push the clearing button on a single-hose regulator, but you have to inhale from the mouthpiece of a double-hose model. Keep the valve closed tightly when the tank is empty. Otherwise, contaminants may enter it.

Handle the tank as though it were packed with TNT whenever it is even partially filled with

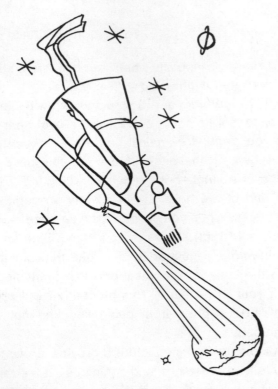

Handle your equipment with care.

air. It is potentially explosive. The energy stored in a filled scuba tank is enormous. A standard scuba tank filled to 2,250 psi contains enough energy to propel a one-ton package more than 160 feet into the air! Scuba tanks should be held securely in place when they are being transported. Prop your diver's bag against your tank or chock your tank with a weight belt to prevent it from rolling. Always lay it down. Some tanks are equipped with boots for standing them up, but the boots do not give tanks enough stability to withstand being brushed against or a boat's rolling and pitching. When you put your tank in the trunk of a car, place the valve toward the rear of the car. In this position, it will not be damaged in the event of a sudden, short stop.

Donning Your Equipment

There is a preferred sequence—with some allowable variations—for donning your skin and scuba gear. Even before you begin to don your gear, lay it out in proper order on the deck (or beach) so that you will not have to fumble to find it. If you use a wet suit, put it on first. Donning your wet suit, in diving terminology, is called suiting up. Put on your safety vest and double-check to be sure it is loaded with a carbon dioxide cartridge. Make sure the pull string is easily accessible. Strap your knife sheath to your right calf if you are right-handed or to your left calf if you are left-handed. Strap your depth gauge and watch to the same wrist. Put on the tank back pack. Then put on the weight belt, making sure that it will not get fouled by your back pack harness if you have to ditch it. Put on the fins. Antifog your mask, but place it on your forehead if it will be more than a few minutes before you go into the water. Use your snorkel for the initial swim along the surface. You will learn how to interchange your snorkel and regulator mouthpiece without removing your head from the water.

Almost all metal parts used in diving equipment are corrosion resistant, but they are not corrosionproof. Wash your gear with clean, fresh water after each day of diving and let it dry in the shade before you pack it away. Do the same with the rubber items, because they can collect salts and organic materials.

Getting Used to Scuba

Take a few minutes to grow accustomed to breathing with scuba before you begin to learn the skills. In waist-deep water breathe as normally and rhythmically as you can. There is no need to take deep breaths and hold them. In fact, you should not. Breathe normally at all times. Do not hold your breath—particularly when you rise to the surface. It is all right to swim along the surface at this point but do not go more than a few feet below the surface until you have learned how to handle yourself.

Clearing the Mask

There are several different ways to clear a face mask if it has become flooded or if some water has trickled into it. The methods you use depend on the type of mask you have—whether or not it is equipped with a purging valve. Regardless of the type of mask you have, you can clear it of water by blowing air through your nose. The air will force the water out if you do it correctly.

With simple masks, press the uppermost part of the mask against your face and, with your head tilted toward the surface, exhale through

You must learn to clear your mask of water easily and quickly. Practice it until it becomes second nature.

Photo by Hank Frey

your nose. You can also clear your mask while you are swimming by rolling over to one side or the other. Again, hold the uppermost part (toward the surface) of your mask firmly against your face and blow. It will take two or three attempts to clear a completely flooded mask.

Masks with nose purge valves are cleared by blowing through your nose with your head tilted either vertically or downward. It is difficult to clear anything more than a slow trickle from masks with small valves. If a mask with a small purge valve becomes completely flooded, hold your hand over the valve and clear your mask as though it did not have a valve. Large purge valves can be used to clear flooded masks or small amounts of water.

Practice clearing your mask in shallow water by pulling the skirt of the mask away from your face and allowing it to fill halfway with water. After you have mastered this, remove and replace the mask under water until you can do it with ease.

Clearing the Mouthpiece

Suppose your mouthpiece came out of your mouth during a dive. What would you do? If you lose your mouthpiece before you exhale the air in your lungs, just put it back in your mouth and exhale into it. This will force the water through a nonreturn valve and you can then resume breathing normally. It is easier to clear the mouthpiece of a double-hose regulator by turning your left cheek downward because the exhaust hose is on your left. It does not matter what position you assume with single-hose regulators.

If you have no air in your lungs to clear your mouthpiece, you can use some of the air in your tank to do it. Single-hose regulators are equipped with a button just for this purpose. You merely replace the mouthpiece while you hold your breath, push the button for a few seconds,

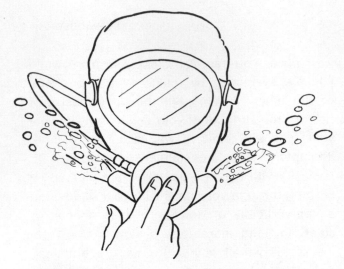

Practice clearing your mouthpiece in waist-deep water until you can do it quickly and smoothly.

If the mouthpiece of a double-hose regulator comes out of your mouth, roll onto your back and you will find it directly over your face.

Single-hose regulators are equipped with clearing buttons.

One way to clean a double-hose regulator is to raise the mouthpiece slightly higher than the regulator body.

Photo by Hank Frey

You can retrieve the mouthpiece of a double-hose regulator by turning to face it.

and then inhale. With a double-hose regulator, you must hold the mouthpiece slightly higher than the regulator body. The mouthpiece will then be subjected to lower water pressure and air will flow freely out of it. Bring the mouthpiece down to the level of your mouth, put it back into your mouth quickly, and inhale.

If a few drops of water remain in your mouthpiece despite your efforts to clear it completely, just swallow the water. It is far better to swallow a little water than to choke on it.

Swimming with Scuba

You get the maximum time from your air supply when you swim slowly and rhythmically. You require more than three times as much oxygen to swim at a fast speed as you do when you are swimming slowly. Furthermore, you risk over-exerting yourself if you maintain a fast speed for too long.

Try to swim in a relaxed manner. Use a slow flutter kick and hold your hands straight out in

Shaney Frey swims slowly and rhythmically to conserve her air supply and her energy.

Photo by Hank Frey

front of you or trail them loosely at your sides. You will not derive much extra speed by stroking with your arms; your fins will give you all the thrust you need. Use your arms while swimming only when you want to change direction.

Interchanging Mouthpiece and Snorkel

Your snorkel is basic equipment whether you skin dive or scuba dive. It serves two purposes in scuba diving: it allows you to conserve your air supply while swimming on the surface; and, after you have run out of air, it permits you to swim back to the beach or to your boat with minimum effort.

Some scuba divers prefer to fasten their snorkels to their mask straps. Others tuck their

Use your snorkel on the surface to conserve air. Dive, remove the snorkel, and change to the regulator mouthpiece.

A convenient way to enter the water from small craft is simply to roll off either backward or sideways.
Photo by Paul Tzimoulis, Skin Diver Magazine

snorkels under the straps of their knife sheaths. Snorkels fastened to mask straps are more likely to get in the way when you are scuba diving but they are less likely to get lost. Suit yourself on this point.

Unless you dive straight down as soon as you enter the water, swim along the surface using your snorkel. Then, when you are ready to dive, remove the snorkel and replace it with your regulator mouthpiece. Reverse the procedure at the end of a dive. You already know how to clear your snorkel and how to clear your regulator mouthpiece. Practice switching from snorkel to mouthpiece and back again.

A Few Words of Caution

The skills up to this point can be learned in shallow water, no more than waist-deep. But learning additional skills that require diving in deeper water means that you will have to equalize the pressure on your ears. Clear your ears the same way you would if you were skin diving. If there is any difference at all, it will probably be easier to clear them when you use scuba. Remember, if you have any difficulty, rise a few feet and try again.

Overexpansion of your lungs can happen if you hold your breath as you ascend (see Chapter

Three). To avoid this, always breathe normally or, if your equipment malfunctions, exhale all the way to the surface. You can suffer an air embolism or any of the related accidents even in less than 6 feet of water. So do not take any chances. Never hold your breath while ascending.

Entering Deep Water

You enter the water from a beach the same way you do when you are skin diving. Walk in backward. Entering water more than about 8 feet deep with scuba is also similar; you can either use the feetfirst entry or roll off the side of the boat. Be sure to hold your mouthpiece and your mask firmly in place with one hand. Never attempt fancy, somersault dives with scuba—you might injure your spine or skull.

Buddy Breathing

Buddy breathing, two people breathing from the same regulator, is a lifesaving skill. It is easiest to do when both you and your buddy are vertical. Divers who must resort to buddy breathing are usually headed for the surface anyway.

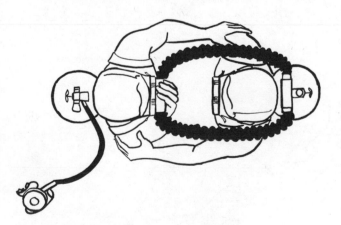

Buddy breathing is an essential skill. To keep the space between you at a minimum, hold on to each other in a dancing position.

Single-hose regulators are equipped with neck straps that have snap-type catches. You must be able to remove your neck strap with one hand —and quickly—in case you and your buddy have to share your mouthpiece. Practice this under water.

The main idea is to keep the distance between you at a minimum and to pass the mouthpiece back and forth smoothly. Neither of you should monopolize the mouthpiece so long that the other begins to feel starved of air. Take one breath—two at the most—and pass the regulator to your buddy. It is best to hold each other in a dancing position while you buddy breathe. This keeps you together close enough so that you do not inadvertently pull the mouthpiece out of one another's mouth. Rise slowly because you will be forced to hold your breath for short periods. Take turns being the host. Practice this until you have it down pat.

Ditching and Donning

Ditching and donning, in diving parlance, means removing and replacing your scuba gear under water. It is highly unlikely that you will ever have to do this. This exercise is really meant to teach yourself how to perform a complex function that requires both skill and concentration. Do not be discouraged if it takes more than several attempts for you to ditch and don with ease.

Swim to the bottom of the deep end of the pool. Sit on the bottom or kneel on one knee, whichever is more comfortable. Remove your weight belt and drape it over your leg. Unfasten your back pack. If you use a double-hose regulator, pull the tank off directly over your head. You can remove a single-hose regulator the same way or you can slip out of the harness sideways. Take a final breath from the tank and turn off the valve. Lay the tank on the bottom, being careful not to bang the valve against the tiles. Start rising slowly to the surface and exhale all

(top) Ditching.
(bottom) Donning.

the way up. Do not hold your breath. Blow air out all the way up to the surface. It may seem strange to you but this can be done even from more than 300 feet of water. Ascending in this manner is called making a free ascent. Rest for a while after you reach the surface.

Surface dive to your scuba gear. Pick up the weight belt first and place it over a leg or, temporarily, across an arm. Raise your tank off the bottom so that the valve is at about the same level as your mouth. If you use a double-hose regulator, hold the mouthpiece at the same level as the regulator body and open the tank valve. Raise the mouthpiece slightly higher than the regulator body for an instant to allow a free flow of air. Quickly lower the mouthpiece and put it in your mouth. Exhale into it with the exhaust hose, on the left, tilted downward. This will make purging any water from the mouthpiece very simple. Donning with a single-hose regulator is even simpler. It does not matter how far above or below the mouthpiece is from the tank valve and regulator body. Open the valve and insert the mouthpiece. Exhale into it and begin breathing from it. You can push the clearing button for an instant before you begin to breathe. This will clear any water in the mouthpiece.

Now that you have air to breathe, you can take your time completing the exercise. Lay the tank directly in front of you with the valve pointing toward you. Position the harness straps so that they will not become tangled. Reach through the shoulder straps and grasp the tank. Rotate it straight over your head and onto your back. The straps should fall into place. Fasten the harness. Finally, put your weight belt around your waist.

Prepare for Emergencies

Your scuba diving skills should become second nature with practice. To be sure that you will be able to cope with unexpected situations, do the following exercises in a swimming pool with your buddy diver or with a group of divers.

Have someone pull your mask off when you do not expect it. This is the way it could happen in open water—and it most likely will at some time. Pretend you are out of air by pointing to your regulator and then moving your hand, palm downward, from side to side. Your buddy should come to your aid quickly and offer you his mouthpiece. Swim at least two lengths of the pool while you buddy breathe. Then do it again without wearing your masks.

Exchange scuba and masks with your buddy. Then, if there are more than two of you, sit in a circle and pass your masks around. Hand your mask to the person on your right and receive a mask with your left hand. Put it on. Clear it. Take it off. Pass it to your right. Repeat this until you get your own mask back again. This is good training especially if you have to clear more than one type of mask.

Drop your mask at one end of the pool. Swim to the other end and back. Put your mask on and clear it.

Remove all your equipment, even your fins, at the deep end of the pool. Make a free ascent. Dive down. Don your scuba. Replace and clear your mask. Put your weight belt and fins on. Ascend, breathing from your mouthpiece. Just as you reach the surface, remove the mouthpiece and replace it with your snorkel. Clear the skorkel and swim away.

If you learn to dive in an indoor pool, turn off the lights so that you can get used to diving in dark water. If you use an outdoor pool or if you cannot turn the lights off for some reason, black-out your mask by putting dark paper inside it. Swim at least two lengths of the pool with near-zero vision.

Have your buddy turn off your air when you least expect it to happen. Turn it back on or, if you cannot reach the valve, make a free ascent. Do not forget to exhale all the way to the surface.

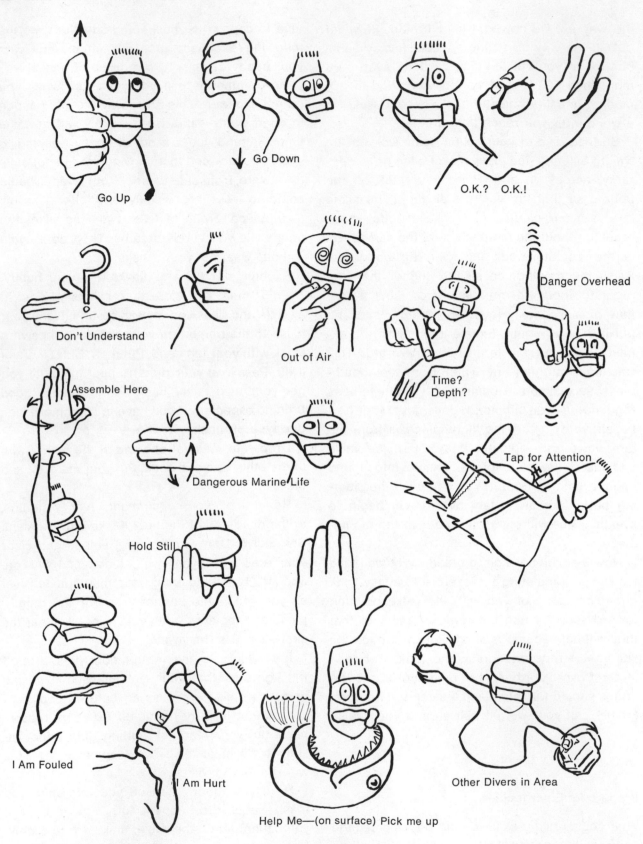

Hand signals.

Scuba diving is a family sport. The Freys prepare to enter the Long Island surf with the help of their daughter, Kathleen. Proper training and practice will allow you to spend many safe and exciting moments beneath the waves.

Photo by George Field

Communication

Communicating with your buddy divers is extremely difficult, because you are limited to hand signals under water. Manufacturers have offered a variety of electronic, wireless communications units, but none of these units works well with scuba. It is difficult to understand a diver even when he uses the most expensive wireless apparatus.

Plan your dives beforehand as thoroughly as possible. Then you will need a minimum of communication under water. Tap on your tank with a hard object or with your knife to attract your buddy's attention if he is not looking your way. Then you can use any of the following hand signals and you can innovate additional ones as required.

Thumb up—go up.

Thumb down—go down.

Thumb and first finger joined in a circle—O.K., I understand.

Arm out to side, palm up—I do not understand your signal.

Point to mouthpiece and wave hand sideways—Out of air.

Point to wrist—What is the depth? What is the time?

First finger of right hand pointed up, move arm up and down—Danger overhead.

Right arm straight overhead, rotate in circle—Assemble here.

Right arm out to side, rotate in circle with palm out—Dangerous marine life.

Right arm held straight up, palm out—Help me, pick me up (surface).

Arm straight in front, palm out—Hold still.

Slashing motion across throat—I am fouled.

One hand clutching throat—I am hurt.

Check List

Before you venture off into open water, get into the habit of checking your equipment and your procedures. Make sure that you have not overlooked anything.

Breathe normally while you ascend. Do not hold your breath.

Dive with a buddy and stay with him at all times.

Wear a safety vest.

Avoid decompression dives.

Avoid overexertion.

Do not allow yourself to become severely chilled.

Use filtered compressed air only.

Put your weight belt on last. Do not overweight yourself.

Use safety release hitches.

Carry a snorkel and a well-sharpened knife.

Check your tank pressure before and after dives.

Tow a diver's flag or display one from your boat.

Have your regulator checked by a qualified repairman at least once a year.

Dive from a float or a boat whenever possible.

Repair your wet suit the night before.

A california diving meet with scores of scuba divers.
Activities such as this are nation wide.
Photo by *Paul Tzimoulis*, Skin Diver Magazine

Veteran diver Jim Turner peers through a crevice in
Molasses Reef off the Florida Keys.

Photo by Hank Frey

6 | Advanced Scuba Activities

The more advanced forms of scuba diving include offshore diving from boats, deep diving, cave diving, wreck diving, diving under ice, and search and recovery. All of these require a significant amount of knowledge and skill beyond that required for simple underwater exploration. You must have many hours of experience before you engage in any one of these activities.

Although the rewards of the more ambitious endeavors are boundless, there are also petty inconveniences and starkly hazardous predicaments: long days, up at dawn and home at dusk; long, boring boat rides with occasional rough seas and seasickness; finding yourself lost and alone inside caves and wrecks; and having your path to the surface blocked—to mention just a few. The dangers can be greatly reduced, if not eliminated, by following safety procedures and by using cool judgment at all times. Your safety and the safety of your buddies always comes first; and anything else is far less important. Never go too deep or stay too long for the sake of accomplishing some task. It just is not worth it.

There are three principal aspects of advanced diving to consider: scuba equipment, safety equipment, and safety procedures. Beyond these general considerations, each form of advanced scuba diving has its own set of precautions.

Scuba Equipment

Begin each dive with a full tank or with one that is nearly full. Running out of air during an "advanced" dive can be dangerous as well as frustrating. Use a J valve (constant reserve). You can reach the surface with ease with a J valve but, even more important, you can descend before you start for the surface if you must. It is sometimes necessary to go deeper in order to exit from a cave or a wreck.

An underwater pressure gauge, although not essential, will help you to keep track of your air supply. An underwater pressure gauge is like the gas gauge on your car: it lets you know how much air is left but not how many minutes of diving time you have. There are too many variables involved for that.

Always plan your dives within the no-decompression limits. It is wise to use double tanks so that you will always have an excess of air just in case. If you exceed the no-decompression limits for unforeseen reasons, the excess air can be used for decompression. As an extra measure of safety, some divers carry an extra "get-home bottle"—a small tank and regulator.

Safety Equipment

Safety equipment includes lifelines, shot lines, underwater lights, diving ladders, and surface floats. Lifelines are vital to safety whenever you enter caves or wrecks or whenever you dive under ice. Use manila or nylon rope at least ¼-inch in diameter. The lifeline can be either tied around your waist or fastened to a ring on your belt.

The shot line is used as a guide for descending and ascending. Its diameter is not critical, but it is easier to get a handhold on large-diameter rope than on a small one. The bottom end of the shot line must be sufficiently weighted so that you and your buddies can pull yourselves down and not pull the weight off the bottom. You need to be just a few pounds heavy at whatever depth you intend to explore. Therefore, if you wear a wet suit, you will be buoyant near the surface by 10 pounds or more. Allow about 15 pounds of weight for each diver using the shot line at the same time.

Lights are invaluable for diving in deep, dark waters or for entering caves and wrecks. Unfortunately, they are not fail-safe. Batteries and bulbs might burn out at the most critical moments. Surface-powered lights are susceptible to cable rupture as well as to burned-out bulbs. A spare light is good insurance.

A well-designed ladder is extremely important for offshore diving. You can do without one only if your diving boat has a very low freeboard, one that is less than a foot high. The diving ladder should extend at least 2 feet below the surface to make it convenient for you to climb aboard when you are fully equipped. The angle between the ladder and the boat should be at least 20 degrees so that your center of gravity is shifted forward. It will also be easier to climb aboard with fins on if you must.

An inner tube or other large float should be tied about 50 feet behind your boat. If, for some reason, you let go of the shot line and drift with the current, the float will provide a resting place and the line will help you to combat the current.

Safety Procedures

Accidents that have occurred during advanced scuba activities have, without exception, resulted from improper safety procedures or from a total lack of safety procedures. The planning and coordination of advanced dives require the cooperation of all the participants, including the boat skipper and his mates. The following recommendations are based on many years of safe and successful advanced diving.

A safety line is essential whenever you enter a wreck or a cave, dive under ice, or dive at night.
Courtesy Skin Diver Magazine

Shaney Frey descends a boat ladder with her fins off.
This is a safe and practical procedure.
Photo by John E. Hopkins, New York City

Diving from boats requires a solid anchorage, someone aboard at all times, and a diver's flag on the mast whenever anyone is under water. A solid anchorage is important because if your boat slips anchor you can drift far from the diving site and endanger the divers below who rely on you. Boats left unmanned during dives have frequently drifted out of sight, and no one is in condition for a marathon swim back to shore after a hard dive.

If there are more than four divers, choose a dive master to take charge of the day's planned diving procedure. He can be a different person on each trip; your group or club can rotate the responsibility. The dive master assigns buddy teams, schedules dives, keeps track of who is in the water, records the before and after tank pressures, and keeps a record of each diver's bottom time. (This information should be recorded with a grease pen on a large piece of plastic kept in plain view.)

At least one team of stand-by divers should be suited up and ready to go over the side at an instant's notice. The buddy teams can take turns standing by. During the final dive, the stand-by divers must have at least five minutes of bottom time remaining and sufficient air in their tanks. This means that they will have to forgo using up all their bottom time, but this is a small enough sacrifice to make.

Limit the number of people in the water to four divers per ladder. A higher ratio would be dangerous if a shark swimming on the surface triggered a mass exodus of divers from the water; it would take too long for all of them to get out of the water.

Surface tenders can assist divers going over the side and coming back aboard. Making it easier for a diver at the surface means that his energy will be conserved to cope with problems under water. A surface tender is essential when lifelines are in use. He must hold the lifeline in his hand continuously to receive and to transmit rope signals.

A pair of underwater tenders are needed whenever you go into wrecks or into caves. The tenders remain outside and pay out the lifeline. This precaution alone could have saved the lives of divers who have gotten lost inside caves and wrecks. The rope signals in Table 2, adopted by the U.S. Navy, are used for surface tending but some can be used for underwater tending too.

Table 2. Rope Signals

Number of Pulls	Tender to Diver	Diver to Tender
1	Are you all right?	I am all right.
2	I am giving you slack.	Give me slack.
3	I am taking up your slack.	Take up my slack.
4	Come up.	Haul me up.
2-2-2		I am fouled and need help.
3-3-3		I am fouled but can clear myself.
4-4-4		Haul me up immediately.

Deep Diving

Limit your dives to a depth of 130 feet. Do not exceed the no-decompression limits except in emergencies. This will minimize the dangers of nitrogen narcosis and the bends. Memorize the no-decompression limits (see Chapter Three). Also memorize, before each dive if necessary, the decompression stops required if you have to exceed the no-decompression limit corresponding to the bottom depth. (Decompression tables for making single dives and for making repetitive dives are reproduced in Appendix C.)

A shot line is important in deep diving. With it, you can control your rate of ascent and maintain the appropriate depth for decompression.

Cave Diving

There are many caves, particularly in central and northern Florida, that beckon "underwater spelunkers." They may satisfy a thirst for exploration but they are hazardous. Lifelines and lights are the order of the day.

Cave diving can be very dangerous because

Limit your dives to no deeper than 130 feet. These scuba divers examine a deck gun on the USS San Diego, *110 feet deep off New York. This was photographed for* Life *magazine.*

Photo by Hank Frey

your direct path to the surface is usually blocked and there are often narrow passages and strong underground currents. Also, it is easy to get lost in a mazelike cave, and cave-ins do happen.

Limit your excursions into caves both horizontally and vertically. Always be in a position to make a free ascent after swimming no more than about 20 feet horizontally. Some cave divers get through small openings by taking off their scuba and shoving it through in front of them. This is a dangerous practice. It means that you have to do the same thing to get back out, and you probably would not have time to do this if you were in trouble. If a passageway is too small for you and your equipment, do not attempt to go any farther. Don't enter caves that have more than a slowly running current. It is hard enough

to battle currents in open water, but currents in caves are terribly dangerous. Your lifeline is your only guide to retrace your route from the cave entrance. Be on the lookout for unstable sections that might cave in.

There have been divers who have drowned for no apparent reason. Their tanks contained enough air to reach the surface safely. In most cases, the divers were found in the water with the mouthpieces dangling. Although there is no definite proof, it was Admiral Momsen's belief that these divers surfaced inside a cave where there appeared to be an air pocket. But the pocket contained not air but noxious gases. The diver removed his mouthpiece, breathed the gas, lost consciousness, fell back into the water and drowned.

Cave explorers, with lights and a lifeline, advance slowly and cautiously.

Photo by Hank Frey

Shaney Frey enters the cave in Crystal River, Florida. This is one of the safest caves to dive in.
Photo by Hank Frey

Wreck Diving

Finding wrecks is perhaps the most time-consuming part of wreck diving. But you can usually leave this to the boat skipper. Wrecks are found offshore, usually more than a mile from the beach. Therefore, you will be subjected to various sea conditions—wind waves, swell, and tidal currents. Wind waves and swell make it difficult for a diver at the surface and, for those on the boat at anchor, rolling and pitching can cause seasickness. If you are particularly susceptible to seasickness, get suited up even before you drop anchor and get into the water soon after. As soon as you are deep enough to get away

Burton McNeely, famed underwater photographer, examines the wreck of a 19th-century ship off Islamorada, Florida.
Photo by Hank Frey

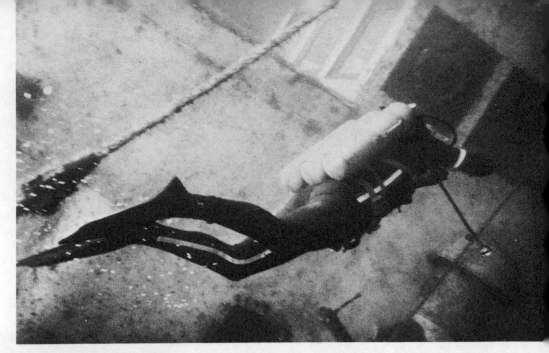

Always approach a wreck from the down-current side. Dick Hillsinger glides past the bridge of the Dutch freighter Pinta *off New Jersey.*
Photo by Michael A. de Camp, Morristown, New Jersey

Herb Cutting pauses at a hatch cover on the Pinta. The ill-fated ship rests on her side in about 85 feet of water.

Photo by Hank Frey

Exploring a wreck from outside is not dangerous if the current is weak and there are no jagged or sharp projections.

Photo by Hank Frey

from the surface motion, you will no longer feel ill. But do not dive if seasickness incapacitates you to the degree that you cannot perform safely. At the bottom you will be faced with currents—tidal and others—which can sap your strength. A current of one knot is rapid for a diver. Try to plan your dives around slack water rather than when the tide is ebbing or flooding.

All wreck diving is not the same. It depends on whether you dive on the more shallow wrecks in subtropical waters or on the deep ones in northern waters. The wrecks themselves even look different. Old wooden wrecks in subtropical waters are generally spewn over large areas after many years of being battered by hurricanes. The wood is at least partially destroyed by toredo worms. Northern wrecks are usually more intact if they were not broken up badly when they sank. The northeast coast of the United States is dotted with thousands of wrecks, dating from the mid-1700s to modern times. Many of the big ones are nearly intact and provide fantastic diving, artifact collecting, and underwater-photography opportunities.

Always approach a wreck from the down-current side. If you approach with the current at your back, you could be swept against the wreck and possibly impaled on a sharp projection. Wear wet suit mittens or heavy gloves to ward off cuts and scrapes.

Exploring a wreck from outside is not dangerous if the current is weak and the wreck has few jagged or sharp projections. But entering a wreck, particularly a large one, can be the most dangerous thing to do under water—with the exception of tormenting a shark. Even on the surface, large ships seem like a maze the first time you go aboard. It is easy to get lost. Under water, it is almost certain that you will get lost in one. It has happened, too often. Never enter wrecks without a lifeline, underwater tenders, a light, and a spare light. Even then, do not enter very far. You must always be able to swim far enough horizontally and while holding your breath to make a free ascent to the surface.

The interior of a wreck might provide excellent visibility but your air bubbles and fins will stir up whatever silt there is and you will suddenly find yourself engulfed in a cloud. When this happens, your light and even your sight becomes almost useless. Your lifeline is then your only guide to escape.

Diving Under Ice

There are very few good reasons to dive under ice. But, like mountain climbers, divers do not always have to do things for a practical purpose. Exploration can be an end in itself.

Ice diving requires surface tenders, lifelines, and adequate thermal protection. A good safety

There are very few good reasons for diving under ice. This diving scientist observes Weddell seals under 8 feet of ice at Antarctica.
Photo by Michael A. de Camp,
Morristown, New Jersey

procedure is to keep the hole in the ice in view at all times.

Limit your underwater time so that you do not become severely chilled. Water under ice is uniformly cold from top to bottom within a few weeks after the surface freezes. Severe chilling can cause you to lose grip strength, swimming strength, and manual dexterity and can impair your mental processes.

Search and Recovery

Finding and retrieving objects under water can be done both for pleasure and for profit. Finding an object is generally much more difficult than retrieving it. Sonars with chart recorders are often helpful if the object of the search is larger than a telephone booth. A practical way to search under water is to employ the distance line—¼-inch rope about 50 feet long tied either to a 20-pound weight or to the anchor line. The search is conducted by swimming in ever-widening circles until you swim the final circle at full line length.

An alternative search method is to form a grid by laying out weighted lines on a section of the bottom. You search each grid methodically before you go on to the next one.

Lifting objects to the surface is usually simple. Divers' lift bags are commercially available and can be used for objects weighing up to 1,000 pounds in water. Although more cumbersome to handle than lift bags, 55-gallon drums are useful as salvage pontoons. They should be flooded and secured to the object with the open end

The authors employed a distance line to scour a shipwreck site off the Florida Keys. Lou Barlia lifts the "gooseneck" from an old sailing vessel aboard the Lady Eleanor.

Photo by John E. Hopkins, New York City

Lift bags make it simple to get heavy objects to the surface. These divers are removing "goodies" from the Pinta.

Photo by Michael A. de Camp, Morristown, New Jersey

down, then filled with air from a spare scuba tank by just opening the valve and letting air rush in. The water in the drums will be forced out by the air. Completely air-filled, such drums exert about 400 pounds of lift.

Bottom suction can be broken by using an excess of lift or by using a "tidal winch" on an object. A tidal winch is made by tying lines to a large surface float or to a boat. The slack in the lines is taken up at low water. Then, when the tide comes in, a lifting force will be transmitted along the lines to the sunken object.

Your underwater excursions will be even more en-
joyable if you acquire a knowledge of marine plants
and animals. These divers examine a beautiful example of antler coral.

Photo by Hank Frey

If you were planning a trip to a foreign country, you would undoubtedly learn as much as possible about its people and its customs. It is just as important for you to learn about the natives of the alien underwater world if your excursions are to be rewarding. Moreover, you will be considerably safer if you understand the behavior of marine life. Despite all the hair-raising tales you might hear about encounters with sharks, moray eels, or giant groupers, you will soon discover that the wet wilderness is largely peaceful and hospitable. You will meet creatures of all descriptions: comical, exotic, beautiful, ugly, and totally bizarre. Among these are the bold and the timid, the active and the sluggish, the immense and the tiny. Some are flowerlike animals that eat fish. Some are fish that resemble plants. The sea's inhabitants perform a varied, colorful hydroshow that cannot be equaled above the surface.

The animal and plant life beneath the surface have evolved virtually free of apparent weight. Consequently, the animals have not developed strong supporting bones and the plants do not have thick, sturdy stems or trunks. Some plants have air bladders, small balloonlike devices that

Among marine animals are those that are immense and bizarre—such as this manatee, or sea cow, being petted by a female diver. This picture was taken with a simple snapshot-type Instamatic camera.
Photo by Tom McQuarrie, Crystal River, Florida

You will meet creatures of all descriptions, such as these sea polyps, which resemble tiny Christmas trees. They can be approached slowly—but if you try to touch one, it will disappear into the coral in a flash.

Photo by Hank Frey

lift them toward the surface. Because of the apparent weightlessness, some sea life grows to gigantic proportions. The blue whale, the largest animal that has ever existed on our planet, may grow to 103 feet and weigh over 119 tons! Many seldom-seen creatures live in the water's depths, where they are subjected to pressure amounting to 1,000 atmospheres, or 15,000 pounds per square inch.

The subterfuges developed for deception, protection, and procuring food are numerous, sometimes humorous, and often unexpected. Perhaps you will chance upon lavishly colored flowers that appear to be growing out of a rock. You pause to ponder over this unlikely circumstance when, before your startled eyes, the lovely, many-petaled blossom grabs a small, unwary fish and gulps it down! Obviously, this flower is not a flower at all. It is, in fact, an animal—the sea anemone. The innocent-looking animal stings its prey, stunning it, and then devours it.

The angler fish or goosefish, is at the other extreme as far as looks are concerned. It is unquestionably a fish, but a preposterously homely one. It is large, 2–4 feet long, drably colored, flat, and flabby. The name "angler" refers to the odd "rod and bait" built in between and forward of the small, close-set eyes. The bait is dangled in front of its enormous Cheshire cat mouth to lure other fish into the mouth as the fish lies partially buried on the bottom. The angler fish also shows surprising speed and hunter's skill when it rises rapidly to the surface and swallows whole ducks and seagulls.

Then there are the porcupine fish and the boxfish, which can quickly convert themselves from

Kelp, largest of the seaweeds, has balloonlike air bladders that hold the plant upright. This kelp forest was photographed off the northwest coast of Mexico.
Photo by Hank Frey

Subterfuges for deception, protection, and procuring food are numerous. The Nassau grouper exemplifies disruptive coloration.

Photo by Owen Lee, Hollywood, California

*A northern sea anemone in the closed position.
Photo by Gordon Groves, Owings Mills, Maryland*

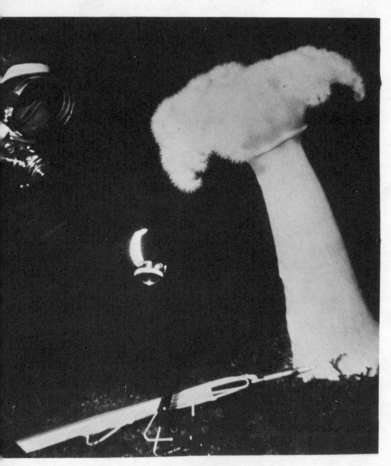

*You can estimate the size of this enormous sea
anemone by considering the size of the diver's head
and his speargun.*
*Photo by Al Giddings, Bamboo Reef of
San Francisco*

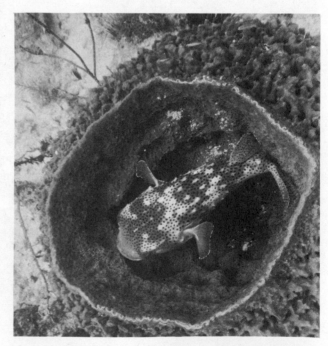

*Camouflaged fish are not difficult to find after you
have an idea of their habits. Do not overlook peering
into things—such as this basket sponge.*
Photo by Hank Frey

Trumpetfish often imitate gorgonian sea whips to avoid detection.

Photo by Hank Frey

ing reports of all verified shark attacks. The panel has done much to disprove the once widely held theory that any shark would attack a man anytime, anywhere, with or without provocation. The facts simply do not bear out this belief.

There is still much to be learned. But what is known will help you to understand how the animals of the water world live and how they react to the presence of a strange animal like you. When you enter their world, you are the alien (imagine how you would react to a Martian in Times Square) with no means of telling the native life that you mean no harm. Also, you are not equipped physically to exist under water. You must rely on your intellect and your equipment to see you safely through your underwater explorations.

Sharks

Of all sea life, sharks probably attract the most attention and curiosity. They may be labeled the vultures of the sea—for sharks are mainly scavengers. However, theirs may be considered a necessary service, because they rid their community of sick and wounded fish and weak stragglers left behind by their own kind. Apparently this is why surface swimmers are in more danger of shark attack than underwater swimmers. Splashing at the surface may sound to a shark like the last struggle of a dying fish—his preferred diet. However, a rogue shark, one that is old or sick or injured, may be driven by hunger to attack a slow and awkward animal such as man. There is on record one confirmed report of a rogue shark that attacked 5 people in 10 days along a sixty-mile stretch of the New Jersey shore during 1916. Such an occurrence is very rare, and of the approximately 350 different known sharks, only a small number are considered dangerous to man.

There is still much to be learned, so it is best to regard all sharks with great respect. Even a

normal-enough animals to inflated, water-filled monstrosities, prickling overall with unappetizing spines. And there is the cowfish, which is awkward and slow-swimming because of its protective shell. The hard shell covers the entire fish, with openings for the eyes, mouth, fins, and tail.

If you are diving in coral waters and see a gorgonian sea whip, take a second, scrutinizing look. You may find that one of the gorgonian branches is actually an upside-down trumpetfish —hanging there trying to look as much as possible like a branch. You will eventually meet these and many others. You might even see things that have never been seen before.

Scientists all over the world are examining all facets of the sea. For an example, since 1959 the Shark Research Panel of the American Institute of Biological Sciences has been compil-

This 12-foot nurse shark, resting under a ledge, is not considered a threat because of its docile nature. Divers are cautioned, however, not to molest any *shark. Even the nurse shark will inflict injury if it is tormented.*

Photo by Paul Tzimoulis, Skin Diver Magazine

small one can do considerable damage if provoked. These animals are not smart and most likely have no idea what you are—much less who you are. They are purely instinctive creatures, literally following their noses to their next meal.

Sharks' highly developed sense of smell is aided by the lateral lines that run the length of the body on both sides and are sensitive to low-frequency vibrations such as those given off by a struggling fish. It is now believed that these senses bring the shark to its prey from a distance, then the sense of sight directs the shark to the kill. Apparently, sharks cannot distinguish either detail or color, but they can single out a

moving target within about 50 feet. Characteristically, as soon as the shark has visual contact it begins what is called the feeding pattern. It circles its prey and moves with increasing speed. The circles tighten until the shark rushes in to grab the fish. At this point the shark is extremely dangerous and will strike at almost anything in the area.

It is of little use—even is foolish—to try to subdue or fight off a shark with your bare hands. Or to try to injure or kill it with your knife or speargun. Pain, as we know it, apparently is not felt by sharks. Also, the shark's skin is covered with thousands of tiny sensory crypts that act as taste buds. Touching the shark may tantalize its appetite and incite it to come back for more. In addition, dermal denticles, or scales similar to teeth, give the shark's body a rough sandpaper texture that can scrape and lacerate your skin. Sharks are tough and superbly designed to exist in a world of water. You are not so designed. The physical advantage is entirely on their side. From your point of view as a diver, sharks are indestructible. Your only advantage is your intellect. And your intellect should tell you that the best prevention against shark attack is not to present yourself as a target in the first place.

Several conditions are believed to influence shark attacks. Time of day seems to be a factor, for more attacks occur at dusk than at any other time of day. Visibility is limited and sharks are actively seeking food at dusk. Poor visibility at any time of day may cause a shark to depend more on the lateral line and less on its vision to lead it to food.

Sharks usually frequent fairly shallow water some distance from the shore, but at night they come into shallower water and are often found inside coral barriers and around docks. The dan-

ger of attack seems to be slightly greater at or near the surface. Although the effect of movement is not clearly established, sharks appear to attack objects that are motionless on the surface as well as objects creating surface disturbances. However, it is generally conceded that splashing and yelling may cause vibrations that can be picked up by the lateral line and attract sharks to you. Blood appears to attract sharks and to incite the feeding frenzy. They are frequently found in areas where refuse is continually dumped. It is not known whether or not they react in any particular or unusual way to human scent. Nearby sharks may be visually attracted by bright, shiny objects and by awkward unfishlike movement.

To minimize the possibility of a shark attack always dive with and stay close to your buddy. Never stray off by yourself and present yourself as a lone target. Sharks have been known to ignore one or more rescuers and continue to attack their original single target. Do not dive in water where dangerous sharks have been sighted. Never tow speared fish under water; put speared fish in the boat or on a float imme-

Common sense should tell you that the best prevention against shark attack is not to present yourself as a target in the first place.

diately. Leave the water at once if you injure yourself and the wound begins to bleed. Never dive when the water is extremely turbid or dirty, and always end your dive at least an hour before dusk. Finally, never tease or torment a shark—no matter how small—and never try to spear a shark.

If you see a shark, leave the water as quickly and as quietly as possible. Swim slowly and smoothly. Keep your eye on the shark as you retreat to safety. Scuba divers should stay underwater until the boat is reached. Do not panic and leave your buddies. Do not turn your back on a shark.

You must take action if a shark closes in before you can get out of the water. Some divers claim to have frightened off sharks by releasing a flood of bubbles, but this is not a reliable defense. As a last resort and with all the strength you can muster, hit the shark on the snout with a shark billy, your speargun, camera, or any hard piece of equipment you are carrying. This aggressive action is outside the behavior of its normal prey and may drive the shark away.

If a shark does attack a diver, it is vital that hemorrhaging be controlled swiftly. Do not attempt to apply a tourniquet. Fill the wound with large gauze bandages and secure them under pressure with elastic bandages. You should assume that the victim is in shock and keep him as warm as possible. Then get him to a doctor without further delay.

The following sharks have been implicated in attacks and are believed to be dangerous:

The *white shark* is a large, powerful, and aggressive animal. It averages about 15 feet but may be up to 20 or 35 feet long. A mature white shark is a pale or lead-white, but the upper body of young ones may be very dark. This shark is found in all warm-temperature and tropical seas but is not commonly found in any one area. It may enter very shallow water in search of food.

The *mako shark* (sharp-nose mackerel shark) is a handsome animal that grows to about 13

White shark.

Mackerel shark.

Hammerhead shark.

Tiger shark.

feet. The dorsal side—or upper body—is deep blue-gray, cobalt, or beautiful ultramarine, and the belly is snow white. The mako is a swift-swimming oceanic species found in the tropical and warm-temperature Atlantic Ocean.

The *mackerel* or *porbeagle shark* is an active and strong swimmer when in search of food but not very active otherwise. It averages about 12 feet in length and is a dark blue-gray on the dorsal side with a white underside. The porbeagle is found in the continental waters of the northern North Atlantic, the Mediterranean, and northwestern Africa to the North Sea, Scotland, the Orkneys, and southern Scandinavia.

The *hammerhead shark* has a truly weird appearance, with its eyes at the ends of hammer-like lobes. The hammerhead is slate to brownish-gray and averages from 8 to 11 feet but may reach 15 feet. This strong, active shark is often seen swimming on the surface in the tropical and subtropical seas it inhabits and is sometimes found inshore, even in tidal or brackish waters.

Shaney Frey found herself eyeball to eyeball with a hammerhead shark shortly after she was directed by her husband to descend and remain perfectly still. The hammerhead, which had come barreling in on the surface, also descended and moved in for a close look. For what seemed an eternity, during which each creature seemed fascinated by the appearance of the other, the shark hung suspended. Then, apparently deciding that this was a particularly unappetizing bit of flotsam, the breath-taking specter disappeared in the murky depths.

The *tiger shark* averages about 12 feet, but specimens have been reported to reach 30 feet. The tiger is gray or grayish-brown on the dorsal side with pale sides and belly. The blotched and striped pattern that inspired its name fades with age. This shark is found throughout the tropical and subtropical belts of all oceans, inshore and offshore. It is usually active only when hunting for food. To add persuasion to this point of view,

a tiger shark, lured to our location by the smell of blood, arrived on the scene shortly after some fellow divers had speared several fish. Hank Frey thought this would be an excellent opportunity to take photos of a tiger shark. But try as he might, he could not get within shooting range of the elusive shark. After a while it became a game of sorts for those on the boat. We shouted and cheered Hank on and indicated what direction the shark had taken, while Hank, manfully plowing on, pursued the ever-retreating tiger. He never did get close enough to take a picture.

The *blue shark* is deep indigo on the dorsal side with a stark white belly. It averages 9 to 12 feet, although infrequently it has been reported up to 20 feet. The blue shark is found in warm-temperate and tropical seas, north to British Columbia in the Pacific and Nova Scotia in the

Peter Gimble, internationally famous diver, finds himself in the presence of a blue shark.
Photo by Michael A. de Camp,
Morristown, New Jersey

The lemon shark is relatively common, particularly in the Caribbean and Florida Keys.
Photo by Burton McNeely, Land O'Lakes, Florida

Atlantic. It is not found in shallow-water areas such as the Gulf of Mexico. This shark is usually sluggish and may be seen basking on the surface. It will follow ships in search of food and is active when hunting but is most active at night.

The *lemon shark* reaches 11 feet and is yellowish-brown on the upper side with a yellow belly. It is found inshore in the western Atlantic from northern Brazil to North Carolina and tropical West Africa. Its habits are not established, but the lemon shark is often found in salt-water creeks, bays, and sounds and may be seen cruising around docks at night.

The *white-tipped shark* grows to 13 feet or larger. Its coloring is light gray or brown or slate brown on the dorsal side and a yellowish or gray-ish-white on the belly and white tips on the fins. This shark is located in the tropical and sub-tropical Atlantic, the Mediterranean and along the Iberian peninsula. It is a slow swimmer and generally sluggish. It is most commonly found in deep offshore waters.

The *black-tipped shark* grows to 6 or 9 feet, and its color cast is blue, gray, or brown with black tips on the fins. Although this is considered a tropical species, it is found north to Massachusetts. The black-tipped shark is an active, swift swimmer and may often be seen leaping from the water.

The *sand tiger shark* reaches 9 feet. It is gray-brown on the dorsal side and grayish-white on the underside and has spots on the sides. The

sand tiger is found in the Mediterranean, tropical West Africa, Canaries and Cape Verdes in the eastern Atlantic, South Africa, and the western Atlantic from the Gulf of Mexico to Florida and southern Brazil. Closely related species are found in Argentine waters and the Indo-Pacific.

There are potentially aggressive animals other than sharks that you should know about and be able to identify.

White-tipped shark.

Killer Whales

The killer whale may be one of the most maligned animals in the sea. This large, intelligent mammal is related to the most popular and publicized marine animal—the bottle-nosed dolphin. It has been considered until recently to be the most dangerous of all underwater creatures. However, the behavior of the killer whale Namu, captured in the Pacific in June 1965 and penned off the coast of Seattle, Washington, does not seem to support that belief. Namu behaved very much like his celebrated cousins. He seemed to enjoy the company of divers who bravely joined him in the pen. But because of the killer whale's size, it must still be considered dangerous to divers even though it may have no intention of causing harm.

The male grows to 30 feet, and the female matures at about 20 feet. Both are jet black on the dorsal side and pure white beneath, with white spots on the side and head. The distinctive dorsal fin is extremely high in proportion to the body. The killer whale is found in all seas but is most common in cold waters. Leave the water at once if a killer whale or a pack (sometimes up to 40) is seen. If you are using a small boat, make a hasty retreat for the nearest shore.

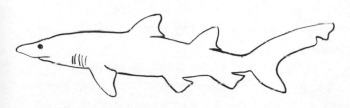
Black-tipped shark.

Sand tiger shark.

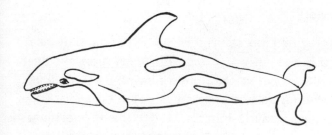
Killer whale.

Barracudas

The great barracuda averages 6 to 8 feet but has been reported up to 10 feet. It is considered dan-

The barracuda is curious and may follow a diver for the entire duration of his dive.
Photo by Paul Tzimoulis, Skin Diver Magazine

gerous because of its enormous teeth. Barracuda are visual feeders and will strike at such bright, shiny objects as a diver's watch. There are more than 20 species of barracuda, and all are swift, voracious carnivores. All but the very small ones such as those found off the California coast are potentially dangerous. They are curious to an unnerving degree and may follow a diver for the duration of a dive. In that case, when no visual stimulus is present, the barracuda will usually scoot away if you face it and let out a loud yell. If you have speared a fish and one or more barracuda go for it, you might try to scare them away, but it is safer to just let them have it.

One afternoon, while absorbed in filming an underwater painting scene, the authors lost track of the time. All afternoon the area had been swarming with an unorganized mass of fish. They intermingled freely and the atmosphere was friendly. A medium-size barracuda had followed us all day. Suddenly, as if one had snapped one's fingers, the atmosphere changed ominously. The change was so sudden and so strong that we felt it immediately. All the fish had, in that moment of change, returned to their family groups. Everywhere, all the animals were completely still, huddled against the protecting coral barriers. The water was filled with tension. Our friend the barracuda was no longer friendly. We had overstayed our welcome—it was well past five o'clock. We knew we must leave at once. But it was not to be so simple a matter. We had an artist's pallette generously burdened with bright oil paints. And our formerly friendly barracuda had dismissed the tastier fish in favor of our color-laden pallette. All attempts to ward off his increasingly aggressive maneuvers were to no avail. He wanted the pallette in no uncertain terms. Finally, in order to reach the boat without a barracuda snapping at our heels, we simply shoved the pallette into its mouth. Today, somewhere off the Florida Keys, is a now middle-aged barracuda with its own set of brushes and a badly warped pallette.

Never try to spear a barracuda. If you fail to kill it, it will defend itself and attack. In either case, the blood will bring others swiftly to the scene.

The upper body of the great barracuda is very dark green, blue, olive, or black, and the sides are a beautiful silver with irregular dark spots near the tail. It is found in the West Indies, Brazil, north to Florida, and the Indo-Pacific from the Red Sea to the Hawaiian Islands. All similar species are found throughout tropical and subtropical waters.

Eels

The *green moray* is large, up to 10 feet, and may be a brilliant green or a brownish-green. It actually has blue skin, but a film of yellow mucus covering its body gives it a green coloring. The green moray is found from Florida to the West Indies and along both coasts of tropical America. Of the more than 20 species of moray, none can be termed as really aggressive, but they will not hesitate to defend themselves if provoked. Then you have a large, tough, slippery opponent equipped with strong teeth that can inflict severe injury.

Morays roam by night and are usually hidden during daylight under rocks and crevices in coral reefs and may be found inshore under bridges and other sheltered places. Never put your hand into a crevice that might house a moray. This would constitute a provocation and bring the moray out to engage you in battle.

The *spotted moray eel* is a smaller species, but it grows to a respectful 3 feet. Its overall coloration may be white, yellowish, or greenish-brown covered with spots. The spotted moray is more active than the green moray and is found from Florida and the West Indies to Brazil.

A related species, the *California moray*, grows to 5 feet and is found from Point Conception to Cedros Island.

The *conger eel* is found from Cape Cod to Brazil. This nocturnal animal grows to 8 feet and may be aggressive. The conger has a green body with a black-edged dorsal fin. This is an oceanic species that should be avoided at all times.

Treat wounds caused by barracudas and moray and conger eels the same as shark bites. While not as severe, the primary concern is still to control bleeding until a doctor can be reached. Contrary to rumored reports, the bite of these animals is not poisonous.

This green moray lives among the rocks off La Paz, Mexico. Morays appear especially formidable because they must "yawn" to pump water through their respiratory system.

Photo by Al Giddings, Bamboo Reef of San Francisco

Sea Snakes

The yellow-bellied sea snake grows to 3 feet and is dark blue-brown above the bright yellow to orange on the underside. This and all other poisonous sea snakes inhabit the tropical Pacific and Indian Oceans. Sea snakes have small cobralike fangs and are considered aggressive and dangerous. They usually live in sheltered coastal areas and the mouths of rivers. They must be avoided.

If a diver is bitten by a sea snake, get him into the boat or ashore and have him lie prone and completely still. Although it is not usually recommended for use in the hands of a layman, a tourniquet should be applied on the thigh for a lower leg injury and above the elbow for injuries of the hand or lower arm. Do not release the tourniquet; keep it in place until you reach a doctor. (This is a recent technique, endorsed by the Red Cross.) Keep the victim in the prone position as you transport him to the hospital. If it is at all possible to do so without injury to yourself, capture the snake so that it can be positively identified. If not, try to give an accurate description to the doctor so that the treatment will be appropriate to the wound. The offending snake may be nonvenomous.

Other Salt-water Hazards

There are, in addition to the potentially dangerous animals mentioned above, many underwater animals that may be dangerous to a diver because of their size, their natural and formidable weapons, and their uneven temperaments. All the following should be given a wide berth, and none should ever be molested in any way.

The *sawfish* may be over 20 feet long, and it has a sawlike weapon it uses to stun and impale fish. *Sailfish, marlin* and *swordfish* all have natural swordlike projections on the snout and have tremendous speed and power. They have been known to attack boats, and in 1967 a swordfish had the distinction of being the only one of its kind—thus far—to spear an underwater research vessel, the *Alvin*. It is easy to see that these, too, must not be tampered with.

Giant groupers or sea bass include the spotted jewfish, the black jewfish, or black grouper, and the California jewfish. These fish are curious (bright objects attract them), fearless, and apparently pugnacious; they have been known to reach 8 feet in length. If molested, a giant grouper will snap or rush at the diver tormenting him with its enormous mouth gaping open. This creates suction as water rushes in the mouth and out the gills. If the mouth is large enough, a diver may be drawn in headfirst down to his shoulders.

The *California sea lion* is not generally considered dangerous if it is not molested. But beware of the mother instinct when young pups are present. The mother can be ferocious when she thinks her pups are threatened. The bull is also quite testy during the mating season and is apt to bite a diver.

Sea turtles, such as the loggerhead turtle, live a very long time and grow very large. They will not attack a diver but will probably bite if cut

Sea turtles grow large. They put up a struggle if molested or cornered.

Photo by Hank Frey

off from an avenue of escape. The male can slash an opponent with the single claw on each of his foreflippers.

Any wounds caused by the animals mentioned above must be treated on the scene according to their severity. First, bleeding must be curtailed. Then infection must be warded off. Treat the victim for shock in all cases. Then get to a doctor as quickly as possible.

The *giant devil ray*, or manta, is black above and white below and reaches up to 23 feet across its winglike fins. While not aggressive, a manta can dismiss a tormentor with one powerful flip of its tremendous fins. Mantas may be seen basking near the surface or leaping clear of the water, falling back with a resounding splash, in tropical and subtropical waters.

There are also nonaggressive marine animals that can cause painful and in some cases, fatal stings. It is your concern to look out for them.

Sea anemones are attractive, colorful animals that look like flowers. They are found attached

Portuguese man-of-war.

Fire coral can be recognized by its smooth surface and mustard color.

Photo by Hank Frey

to coral, rocks, wrecks, and even the shells of living crabs. If you touch one, you will receive a short-lived but painful sting.

Fire coral is not a true coral but lives among and even takes the shape of true coral. It can be recognized by its smooth surface—as opposed to the porous surface of true coral—and its mustard color. The sting inflicted by fire coral is quite intense on contact, causing large red welts. But the pain diminishes and the welts vanish within a few hours.

Elkhorn coral also stings but causes no more than a temporary prickling sensation with no aftereffects.

The *Portuguese man-of-war* and related species can inflict dangerous stings, depending on their size. The blue and pink air-filled sail, or bladder, is carried over the surface by the wind and the currents. The stinging tentacles trail in the water below. Some of the largest ones have tentacles that are 30 feet long. The man-of-war can deflate its sail and sink below the surface when the surface is rough. You must be on the lookout for them in waters they are known to inhabit.

The *sea wasp* is transparent, with a high, almost square bell and four tentacles. A related species has groups of tentacles at the four corners of the bell and is considered the most venomous organism in the sea!

If you have the misfortune of coming into contact with any one of these, the adhering tentacles must be removed quickly with a towel or sand. Apply diluted ammonia or alcohol. If the sting is severe, seek medical aid at once.

Avoid touching a man-of-war or jellyfish that you find stranded on the beach. They can still give you a hefty sting before they decompose in the sun.

There are other stinging jellyfish, and, as often happens, the same species may be known by different names in different localities. It is best to allow all jellyfish plenty of room to undulate in their quiet, relatively peaceful way. Remem-

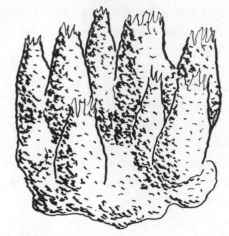

Fire sponge.

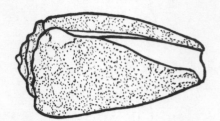

Cone shell.

Scorpionfish.

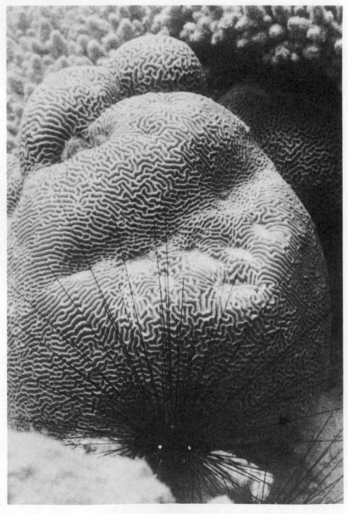

A long-spined sea urchin at the base of brain coral.
Photo by Joep Strolenberg, Holland

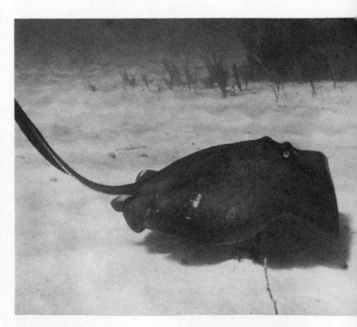

A giant southern stingray with a 5-foot wingspan
glides away from the photographer.
Photo by Hank Frey

One of the most photogenic reefs in the world can be found off Cozumel Island, Mexico. It abounds with marine life.

Photo by Paul Tzimoulis, Skin Diver Magazine

ber, you can't hear them approaching, so you have to actively look out for them.

Both the *fire sponge* and the *poison-bun sponge* inhabit the waters from the Florida Keys to the West Indies. Both inflict severe stings. Always wear heavy gloves if you are going to handle any living sponge.

Long-spined *sea urchins* are common throughout the world. They are generally seen clustered around rocks and coral. They are not stationary (as many people believe) and can navigate slowly from place to place on tiny tubelike feet. They bristle with slender but brittle black needles whose sharp, tapered points penetrate deeply at

the slightest touch. The needle breaks off flush with the surface of the wound, and it is nearly impossible to remove it. Paint the wound liberally with antiseptic. The needle will dissolve in a few days.

Cone shells, intricately and attractively designed, house small animals that can inflict a paralyzing sting. These shells can be recognized by their distinctive conical shape.

The much abused *octopus* is not aggressive by any measure and is, in fact, a cautious, timid animal. But if it is made the target of sport (hunting the octopus is popular in some regions), it may use its parrotlike beak. The bite of an octo-

The porkfish schools densely in shallow waters during the summer. It occasionally pecks at the skins
of larger fish to remove parasites.
Photo by Paul Tzimoulis, Skin Diver Magazine

A school of mullets, headed into the current, hover above the bottom in Crystal River, Florida.
Photo by Paul Tzimoulis, Skin Diver Magazine

pus is venomous and sometimes, though rarely, fatal.

The *spiny dogfish shark*, *ratfish*, *sea catfish*, *scorpionfish,* and *toadfish* all have one venomous spine—or more—which, on contact, can cause painful wounds. The wounds must be cleaned with cold salt water or, if available, with sterilized water. The victim must be kept warm and receive immediate medical care.

Stingrays are not aggressive. When one wounds a diver with the stinger or stingers on its tail, it is usually the result of having been stepped on. If you must walk on the bottom, shuffle your feet to give warning to the peaceable ray, and it will glide out of your way.

If you are wounded by a stingray or any of the above venomous animals, the wound must be squeezed and soaked in water as hot as you can bear (but not hot enough to cause a burn). The hot water will draw out the venom. Go to a doctor at once.

Electric rays are slow, sluggish animals that generate and discharge electrical shocks. The torpedo ray is the most powerful of this species and can discharge up to 220 volts—enough to disable an adult diver.

The *electric stargazer* buries itself in the sand, leaving only its eyes and mouth exposed. The stargazer grows to a foot and is purplish-gray with tiny white spots. It has modified optic nerves that can generate a noticeable shock. Shocks from these animals usually need no treatment.

Plant life can create hazards for the unwary diver as well. Vine kelp grows to 200 feet and bladder kelp reaches 130 feet, so it is best to avoid diving in and perhaps become entangled in beds of kelp. If you dive in a kelp forest, always move forward. You are more likely to entangle your valve and regulator in kelp if you back up. If you become lost, reach above your head and part the weeds. Then surface and look for a clear area. Go below again and swim toward the clearing.

Fresh Water Hazards

The multitude of diversified fish found in lakes, streams, creeks, and ponds include the armored alligator gar, queer paddlefish, bluegill, sunfish, rainbow darter, hogsucker, carp, trout, and, of course, bass. However, in the midst of these game and food fish are a few animals that can be harmful to divers.

The most dangerous fresh water snake is the *water moccasin*, or "cottonmouth." This venomous snake can be recognized by its relatively stout body and by the two pits between its eyes and nostrils. It is found only in the southern states and, fortunately, is not aggressive. If you accidently, or mischievously, corner the water moccasin or molest it, it will attack you in self-defense. In the event of an attack, the victim must be given prompt medical care (see *sea snake*).

Fried *catfish* is indisputedly delicious. But catfish must be handled with great care because of the sharp spines on the pectoral and dorsal fins.

The spines of the madtom and the stonecat are poisonous, and wounds should be treated with hot water soaks until medical care is available.

The water itself can be harmful to you if it is polluted or stagnant. Either of these conditions may cause severe and hard-to-cure rashes or illness.

Above all, whether you dive in sea water or fresh water, learn all you can about the plants and animals in your diving areas. In this way, you will not only arm yourself against possible injury but may even notice some pattern of behavior never seen before. You may actually be able to contribute previously unrecorded information. Organizations such as the International Oceanographic Foundation and the American Littoral Society encourage and organize divers to fill gaps in the knowledge of underwater life. Diving can be more than just a time-filling sport. It can provide a helping hand to scientific research.

A perfect shot with a Hawaiian sling!
Photo by Paul Tzimoulis, Skin Diver Magazine

Spearfishing can be done on the highest level of sportsmanship or it can be wanton slaughter. One very simple rule to keep spearfishing in proper perspective is to shoot only what you intend to eat. It is senseless to shoot fish only to discard them later. From the sportsman's point of view, spearfishing can be one of the most exciting and demanding underwater challenges. You need more than brawn to be a champion. Champion spearfishermen are students not only of spearguns but also of the animals they hunt. Admittedly, luck plays a role. But you need more than good luck to get the wary ones; you need skill and know-how.

Spearfishing laws, where they exist, vary from state to state and are changed from time to time. State diving councils or local dive shops should be able to advise you about local laws. Shooting fish in fresh water—except for carp, gar, and suckers—is forbidden almost everywhere. If you plan to spend weekends or your vacation in a strange diving area, write in advance for information about the local spearfishing laws.

You will probably hear it said, dogmatically, "Never spear fish when you are using scuba." There are justified exceptions to this. Scuba is

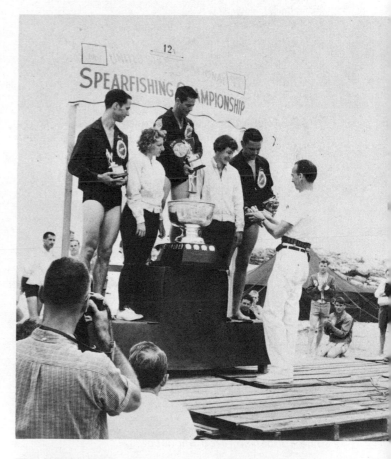

The United States National Spearfishing Championship is one of the major events of the sport.
Photo by Paul Tzimoulis, Skin Diver Magazine

Championship form with a Hawaiian sling.
Photo by Paul Tzimoulis, Skin Diver Magazine

forbidden during spearfishing competitions. It takes very little ability to sit on the bottom and shoot at fish as they swim by. Stalking and shooting fish while you are skin diving is more sporting. However, if you are on a diving expedition and depend on spearfishing for your meals, the use of scuba is justified if you shoot only what will be eaten.

The weapons used in spearfishing range from simple handspears to high-powered spearguns. Some are powered by rubber, some by compressed air, some by carbon dioxide cartridges, and others by a new hydraulic system.

Handspears

The simplest and most economical weapon is the rubber-powered handspear. The shaft is 6 feet or longer and has a rubber sling fastened to the rear. Stretch the rubber by moving your hand forward on the shaft with the rubber between your thumb and your first finger, aim, release the handspear, and let it fly. Reloading is quick and easy so you will be able to take many shots during a dive. The main drawback is that handspears are long and difficult to maneuver. Also, your shooting distance is limited to a little less than the length of the shaft.

Hawaiian Sling

The Hawaiian sling is not really a gun; it is more like an underwater slingshot. It consists of a plastic tube, 6–12 inches long, with a loop of rubber for propulsion. The shaft, about 4 feet long, is placed within the plastic tube, and the end of the shaft and the rubber are gripped together. Stretch the rubber with one hand while you hold the plastic tube with the other, aim, and release. Hawaiian slings are useful only in very clear water, and even then a high degree of skill is needed to use them successfully. It is easy to maneuver a Hawaiian sling and, with a great deal of practice, you can develop deadly accuracy with it.

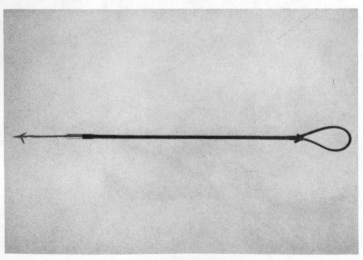

The rubber-powered handspear.
Photo by Hank Frey

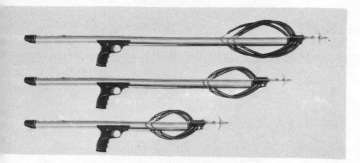

The rubber-powered speargun—or arbalete—is available in various lengths and powers.
Courtesy U.S. Divers Company

Spearguns are pointed rather than aimed. It takes practice to hit a target consistently.

Rubber-Powered Spearguns

Rubber-powered spearguns—or arbaletes—operate on the principle of the medieval crossbow. Of the various types of spearguns, the rubber-powered models are the simplest and, in many situations, the most effective.

The spear shaft is mounted on top of a barrel. Rubber tubing or solid rubber strands are stretched and held in place by metal wishbones. The wishbones are placed in notches on the shafts. The spear shaft is released by pulling a trigger. The shaft remains attached to the speargun by a nylon line.

Rubber-powered guns are available with from one to four rubbers. The four-rubber speargun is more powerful than any other type, but you need high power only for very big game. A double-strand gun will suffice for general purposes. You have your choice of using only one of the rubbers for shooting at close distances or both of them for maximum power. You need only enough power to drive the speartip well into the fish or, at most, just through the fish. If you use too much power, the shaft may go right through the fish and become blunted as it hits the rocks or coral in the background. Keep the safety lever in the safe position until you are ready to fire the spear. Do this with all spearguns.

To load a rubber-powered speargun, place the butt against your stomach and pull back the rubber tubing until it has stretched over the notch in the shaft. Sights on spearguns of all types are useless. You do not really aim a speargun, you point it. It takes a lot of practice to do this accurately.

Most rubber-powered spearguns have hollow barrels, which make them buoyant. Buoyancy is desirable when you have to let go of your speargun. As a skin diver, it is easier to recover things on the surface than it is to dive to the bottom. Buoyancy in rubber-powered guns lends good balance because the handles are usually close to the butts. If you swim rapidly, the rubber strands will oscillate, causing both noise and increased drag. Guns with metal barrels give fish a split-second warning because the air-filled barrels resonate with noise just as the shaft is released. Wooden guns eliminate this resonance.

Pneumatic Guns

Pneumatic guns, as the name implies, are powered by compressed air. The compressed air is

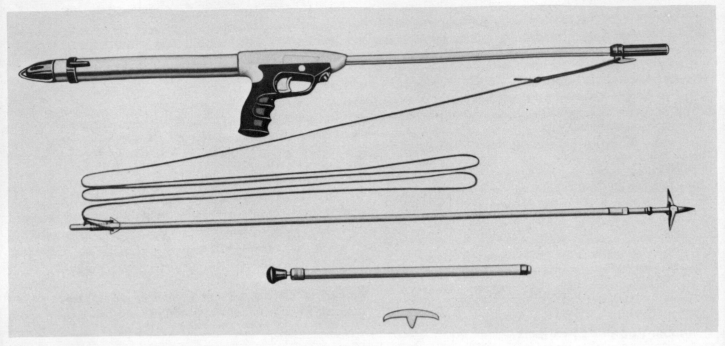

Medium-size pneumatic guns suffice for all but large game.

Courtesy U.S. Divers Company

The Tri-Jet pneumatic gun.

Courtesy Dacor Corporation

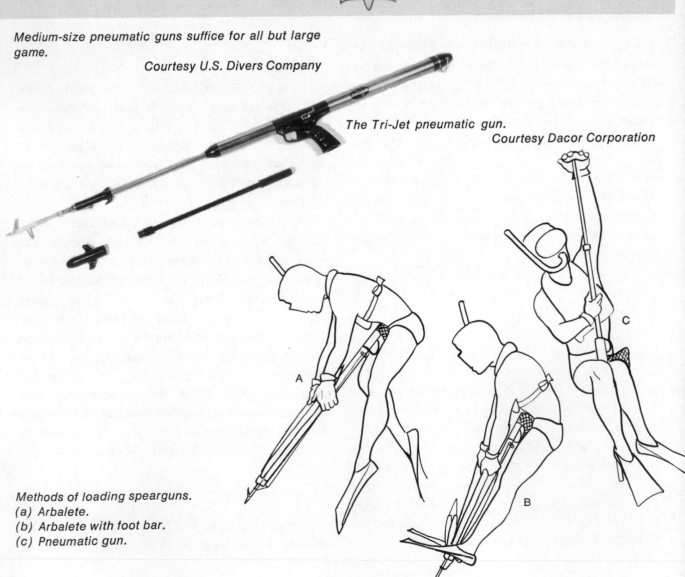

Methods of loading spearguns.
(a) Arbalete.
(b) Arbalete with foot bar.
(c) Pneumatic gun.

sealed in a chamber and does not escape with each shot. It acts like a spring. A separate pump is supplied with each pneumatic gun. You simply pump the compressed-air chamber to obtain the propulsion thrust you desire. It is ordinarily better to have a little too much power than too little power.

The gun is loaded by inserting the shaft all the way into the barrel until it locks in place. Under no circumstances should you ever fire a pneumatic gun out of the water, because the muzzle might be blown off. Water softens the impact.

Pneumatic spearguns are less buoyant than rubber-powered ones and generally have better maneuverability. They are easier to maneuver because the handle is centered along the barrel. You can turn them quickly and their slim profile adds little to swimming resistance.

Other Types of Spearguns

A new type of gun, operating on a hydraulic principle, has been developed by Scubapro. The gun has an aluminum barrel, and all other parts are made of stainless steel. This recent innovation shows great promise. It has good propulsion and accuracy.

Spring-powered spearguns were popular about 10 years ago but they have long-since gone out of vogue. They were long and heavy and required meticulous maintenance. Sand played havoc with spring guns, and the springs, unless properly lubricated, gradually lost power.

Carbon dioxide guns were thought of as underwater "elephant guns." It is true that carbon dioxide guns are extremely powerful, but the power is awfully expensive. The main disadvantage of these guns is that they emit a burst of bubbles and you cannot see the flight of your spear. If you miss the fish, you have no way of knowing whether your shot was high, low, or to one side.

Spearheads

Spearheads are almost universally made of stainless steel to prevent corrosion. It is important to use the proper type of spearhead for the game you intend to hunt. You should choose one that will penetrate the fish and hold him from pulling away.

There are spearheads that remain fixed to the shaft and spearheads that detach after impact but are secured to the shaft by a short length of steel cable. The detachable head makes it nearly impossible for fish to "spin off" the shaft. Some spearheads are equipped with barbs that

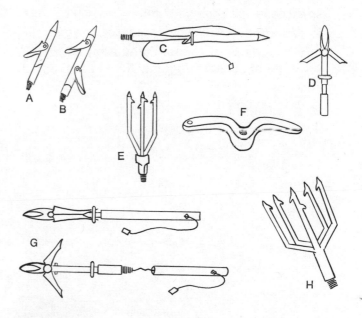

Spearheads.
(a) Single-barb.
(b) Double-barb.
(c) Detachable.
(d) Arbalete.
(e) Trident.
(f) Loading tool.
(g) Double-barb; detachable with three-sided point.
(h) Five-prong.

swing outward as the fish tries to pull away. Barbs that swivel as well as swing outward are best because they follow the fish's movement, preventing him from working free of the shaft. Hexagonally pointed heads penetrate fish better than round points but are more susceptible to damage if they hit against rocks. Round pointed spearheads with replaceable tips are a good choice for hunting along rocky bottoms.

Trident points are used for small fish—up to about 5 pounds. However, they are often difficult to remove without tearing away flesh. A small single-barb spearhead is often a better choice.

Adaptors are available for using a spearhead with one type of thread on a shaft with a different type. European shafts and spearheads use metric threads; those produced in the United States use American standard threads.

Keep an extra spearhead and shaft on hand. Should you miss your mark and hit a rock, the spearhead will become blunted and you will have to change it. A frisky catch can bend your shaft into a modern-art shape. Without replacements, your day of spearfishing may come to an abrupt end.

Shock Cords

Many of the more powerful spearguns are equipped with shock cords to prevent a fish from breaking loose as it stretches the attaching line to its full length. If your gun is not equipped with a shock cord, you can easily make one. Slip a 2-foot length of surgical rubber tubing over the gun end of your attaching line. Tie the end nearest the gun butt by wrapping it tightly with nylon cord. Then stretch the rubber to full length, holding the other end securely. Let the tubing relax but keep a firm grip on the end farthest from the gun butt. The line will curl up within the tubing. Then tie this end with nylon cord.

Techniques

As big Jim Christiansen, an all-time champion, sums it up, a spearfisherman should be observant, slow, lazy, and sneaky. Any fish can swim faster and farther than you can—and he can stay underwater much, much longer. So you will have to be crafty if you want success.

Keep a sharp lookout along the bottom and especially around rocks and other obstructions.

If you get all the way to the bottom and look under ledges . . .

This is what you might see—a tasty grouper.
Photos by Hank Frey

Make quiet, graceful dives.
Photo by Paul Tzimoulis, Skin Diver Magazine

Once you have speared your prey, get it out of the water to avoid attracting unwanted company.
Photo by Paul Tzimoulis, Skin Diver Magazine

Aim just behind the gills.

Photo by Hank Frey

Do not carry fish on a fish ring. Get them into a boat or into a watertight float.

With your gun pointed down and away from the other spearfishermen, you swim along the surface, towing the all-important float and diver's flag. Keep a sharp lookout along the bottom, especially around rocks, undersea obstructions, shipwrecks, and other similar favorite feeding places for fish. Make quiet, systematic dives in order to scour the bottom. You will probably find a wise fish hiding under the protection of an overhang. It is amazing how quickly fish have caught on to the ways of the spearfisherman, and although many flee at the first sign of one, others arrogantly remain just a fraction beyond the range of the speargun. Your skill and patience is put to a severe test. When you spot your evening's meal, stalk it as you would stalk game on land. Make a quiet, graceful dive. Make your movements seem to be caused by water movements. Get as close as you can without alarming your prey, aim just behind the gills and release the shaft. Once you have it speared, get the fish out of the water and into a boat or watertight float so that its blood doesn't attract unwanted company (especially in subtropical wa-

ters). There have been numerous cases reported of sharks stealing fish and in some instances seriously injuring divers.

A very effective and inexpensive way to keep the blood from speared fish from attracting shark and barracuda is to stretch an inner tube around an old washtub and just drop each freshly speared fish into the tub.

Sometimes it is best to hide from your prey and let him stalk you rather than the other way around. Cracks, crevices, and caves in reefs are good hiding places. If you cannot hide all of your body, hide at least part of it. Fish with pharyngeal teeth make characteristic sounds when they eat. The sounds are similar to scratching sounds. So, if you scratch the coral or rocks with your spearhead, you might be able to entice one of these fish to come closer. He will want to get in on the feast. Remain hidden until he gets close enough. Then—*pow.*

Maintenance

After you have spearfished in salt water, your gun should be thoroughly rinsed in fresh water to remove all traces of salt and sand from its moving parts. Disassemble and clean the trigger mechanisms; lubricate them with a light coat of oil. Do not use heavy grease—it picks up sand and grit. Inspect rubber strands for fatigue. Examine the rubber at the muzzle carefully. If it snaps, it could smash through your faceplate and damage your eyes.

Store your shafts without the spearheads attached. The spearheads will remain sharply pointed and can do no damage in your accessory bag. Coat all metal parts lightly with oil but take care not to get any oil on the rubber slings. The rubbers should be powdered.

Safety

The tip of a loaded speargun should never be out of the water. A loaded speargun on the beach, in a boat, or on a float can have tragic consequences. A shaft released in air will hit with the impact of a bullet. Handle your speargun with as much care as you would a firearm—it is a lethal weapon. Keep the spearhead covered when it is not in use.

Swim along the surface with your gun pointed down and away from your buddy. It's your business to know where he is at all times. Shorten the spear line in murky water so that it won't travel beyond visibility. Fire your shaft only when you are sure it will be stopped against a background if you miss your target. Most important, do not fire at anything unless you can clearly identify it as legal prey.

A number of tragic spearfishing accidents have resulted in critical injuries. In one case, a spearfisherman shot his buddy, thinking he was a shark. Although the black suit and turbid water confused the hunter, he should have been absolutely certain of his target. There are no excuses.

The trigger of your speargun should be pressed only after careful deliberation.

Try to do your spearfishing during the incoming tide. Blood from the fish will then be carried toward shore rather than to deeper waters, where you-know-what live. If you work the outgoing tide, be sure to remain up-tide from the speared fish. A shark in quest of food will then see the fish before he sees you—he might otherwise mistake you for his meal. If a shark approaches, let go of your catch and move up-tide with rhythmic motions.

Marine-life experts agree that blood is a strong feeding stimulus to sharks. Low-frequency vibrations given off by struggling fish seem to send out a homing beacon. This is reason enough to get speared fish out of the water immediately. A sturdy plastic bag or a washtub can be fitted in your inner-tube float to hold your catch. If you are working in the area of your boat, get your fish aboard as soon as possible.

A plastic-lined basket or a washtub will keep blood and body juices from becoming a "flavor trail" for sharks.
Photo by Paul Tzimoulis, Skin Diver Magazine

Diver Scott Slaughter blasts a lemon shark with a 12-gauge powerhead.
Photo by Burton McNeely, Land O'Lakes, Florida

Catching "bugs" by hand is a natural adjunct to spearfishing.
Photo by Paul Tzimoulis, Skin Diver Magazine

An underwater movie photographer and a lovely lass
with a still camera capture on film the beauty of
Bahamian waters.

Photo by Owen Lee, Hollywood, California

9 | Underwater Photography

Underwater photography is the most popular pastime among skin and scuba divers. In the past few years, underwater photography equipment has developed enormously so that today you can purchase reasonably priced, well-designed equipment to fill every need. Among the major developments that have simplified underwater photography is the amphibious 35mm camera. This camera, smaller than most 35mm cameras, can be taken underwater without a separate housing. Other advances include a variety of commercial housings for instant-loading cameras, powerful underwater movie lights, and housings for electronic flash units. In addition to the commercially available equipment, there are numerous custom housing manufacturers, or you can try to build your own equipment.

It would be misleading to say that underwater photography is uncomplicated. It takes knowledge, perseverance, and experience to develop into a good underwater photographer. But the rewards are well worth the effort. Besides providing new and different entertainment for your family and friends with underwater photographs, slides, and movies, you can enter one of the many underwater film festivals held throughout the United States each year.

Your choice of equipment will depend upon whether your interest lies mostly in color slides, in prints of still pictures, or in movies. Your choice will also depend on how much you want to spend. You might want to buy a housing for a camera you already own, or you might prefer to start from scratch.

Still Cameras

Cameras used for underwater photography range from inexpensive snapshot cameras to very expensive professional models. Snapshot cameras are equipped with a fixed focus, a fixed aperture (or lens opening), and a fixed shutter speed. They are easy to operate because they require no adjustment of controls, but it is this very simplicity that limits their use to only ideal light conditions. The only remaining variable with snapshot cameras is film speed. Choose the film speed to match the brightness of the light. Snapshot cameras are recommended only for fairly clear, bright water such as swimming pools, springs, and clear ocean water.

Many underwater photographers prefer to use

The Mako amphibious snapshot camera uses 120 roll film.

Courtesy Mako Products, Inc.

Underwater snapshot cameras, although limited in versatility, are easily used by beginners.

Photo by Hank Frey

Doris Tzimoulis steadies herself with one hand while shooting close-ups with an Instamatic camera.

Photo by Paul Tzimoulis, Skin Diver Magazine

35mm cameras with adjustable controls and interchangeable lenses. This choice offers numerous advantages including compact camera size, a large film capacity (36 exposures), relatively economic film cost and processing, the ability to choose the lens that best suits the particular requirements, and the ability to adjust the various camera controls to achieve the best results. Among the 35mm cameras, but in a class all by itself, is the amphibious camera with adjustable controls, interchangeable lenses, a special filter for underwater photography, and a compatible flash unit.

Plexiglass housing and flash for a completely automatic Instamatic camera model.
Courtesy Underwater Photographic Services, Inc

The Nikonos amphibious camera with flash gun and sportsfinder.

Courtesy U.S. Divers Company

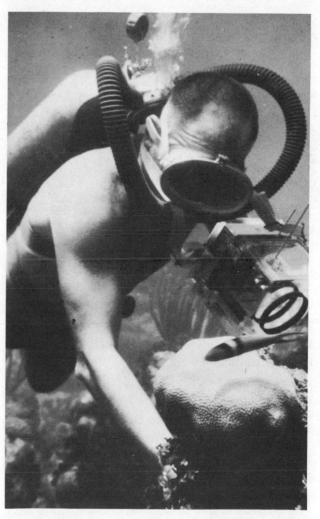

Burton McNeely, a pioneer underwater photographer, using a Hasselblad Superwide-C (2¼″ by 2¼″) in a custom plexiglass housing.

Photo by Hank Frey

The 2¼-inch by 2¼-inch format (120 film) is preferred by some underwater photographers because it provides a larger negative and transparency size. There is definitely an advantage to the larger format in that less magnification is required to make prints and the larger transparencies project much better onto screens. Professionals favor this format because most publishers prefer it. One of the really important assets of using a 2¼-inch by 2¼-inch reflex camera is that you can compose your photographs through the lens, thereby obtaining on film exactly what you see with your eye. These cameras are particularly invaluable for extreme close-up photography. Some single-lens 35mm reflexes can be used in this manner, but they are much more difficult to use conveniently because of the smaller image.

Paul Tzimoulis, editor and publisher of Skin Diver Magazine, *with a Nikon Super-8 movie camera in a Cine Mar housing.*
Photo by J. Barry Herron, Temple City, California

Movie Cameras

The advent of the Super-8 format has really been a boon to underwater photography. Super-8 movie cameras are available with electric eyes that automatically control the exposure and electric drives that expose 50 feet of film without winding. Super-8 movie film comes in cartridges that make loading and unloading quick and easy. Compared to the 16mm format, film and processing are relatively inexpensive. Shortly after the introduction of Super-8 film and cameras, a sizable variety of underwater housings was made available for many of the Super-8 models.

Although the 8mm format is being made obsolete by the larger Super-8 format, it is still possible to purchase camera housings for many of the 8mm models.

If you have any hopes of either entering film festivals or selling footage, you will have to shoot 16mm film, which is considerably more expensive than either Super-8 or 8mm.

Hank Frey with a Bolex 16mm movie camera in a Bolex housing.
Photo by Shaney Frey

A wide-angle lens is the most useful type for general underwater photography. The Nikkor 28mm lens for the Nikonos camera is optically corrected for subsea use.

Courtesy U.S. Divers Company

Lenses

Wide-angle lenses are generally more useful than normal lenses or telephoto lenses for underwater photography. With a wide-angle lens you can get closer to your subject; the decreased subject-to-camera distance results in less turbidity in the path, better contrast, and enhanced brilliance of colors. This is especially Important in turbid water. Another advantage of the wide-angle lens is that it has a greater depth of field, allowing you to operate within a larger range of camera-to-subject distances without adjusting the focus.

To photograph small fish or other small subjects at close range, you will need to use a close-up lens attachment. These attachments enable you to focus your lens for shorter distances than otherwise possible and are available in various powers corresponding to various minimum distances. Some fish, such as barracuda, will not allow you to approach them closely enough to profit from the use of close-up attachments. For the more wary fish, you may want to use a normal lens or even a telephoto lens rather than a wide-angle lens.

Camera Housings

Cast aluminum housings and plexiglass housings are the two most widely used types. The metal housings are more rugged because they have greater impact resistance. However, a well-designed plexiglass housing will give you many years of service if you handle it with care. In general, plexiglass housings cost less than cast aluminum housings. It is possible to see whether or not a plexiglass housing is leaking because the material is transparent. However, cast aluminum housings employing O-ring seals or properly designed gasket seals (such as in the Rolleimarin or the Bolex housing) are highly reliable.

In any camera housing look for compactness, ruggedness, slight negative buoyancy not to exceed 3 pounds, easily operated controls, ease of loading and unloading film, and a reliable framing device.

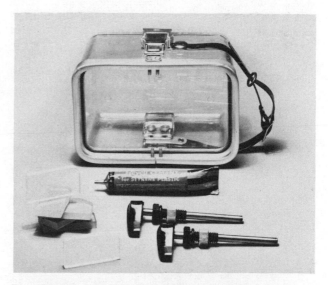

The Ikelite molded camera-housing kit comes in two sizes; one fits Instamatics and many 35mm cameras; a larger one accommodates twin-lens reflex cameras. The controls and camera mount are installed by the purchaser or can be installed by the factory.

Courtesy Ikelite

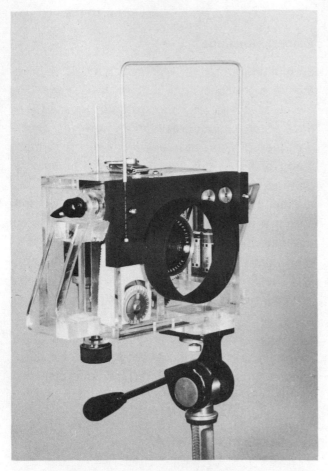

The Cine Mar aluminum housing accepts more than two dozen Super-8 movie cameras. It is well designed and highly reliable.

Photo by Al Giddings, Bamboo Reef of San Francisco

A homemade plexiglass housing for the author's 35mm Robot Royal sequence camera. Complete details regarding housing design and construction can be found in Frey and Tzimoulis' *Camera Below* (see Bibliography).

Photo by Hank Frey

Al Giddings, one of the finest underwater photographers in the world, designed and built this housing and light for the 16mm Kodak Cine Special with a 200-foot film load.

Photo by Al Giddings, Bamboo Reef of San Francisco

The Rolleimarin housing for Rolleiflex cameras is a fine example of good design and rugged construction. A veteran of more than a decade, this combination has been used by numerous award-winning cameramen.

Courtesy Honeywell, Inc.

The Bolex housing has been in use for more than 10 years and is tried and proven.
Courtesy Paillard, Inc.

It is important to maintain equipment properly. Wash it thoroughly with fresh water after it has been exposed to chlorinated water or to sea water. Make sure to flush all salts out of crevices. Lubricate O-rings or gaskets frequently using silicone grease.
Photo by Hank Frey

Among the more sophisticated and higher-priced equipment, the Rebikoff 16mm underwater camera is equipped with a special lens that corrects for distortion under water.
Courtesy Rebikoff Underwater Products, Inc.

Exposure Meters

Exposure meters are extremely useful when using only the available light under water even though they are not absolutely essential. The reflected-light type of exposure meter is much more popular and more accurate for underwater use than the incident-light type. An exposure meter serves the same purpose under water that it does above the surface; it takes the guesswork out of setting camera controls.

Artificial Light

The intensity of daylight is severely reduced with increasing depth either in seawater or in natural bodies of fresh water. As a rule of thumb, you must open your lens one additional *f*/stop for every additional 10 feet of depth. The severe reduction of light under water makes it necessary either to use fast film and wide lens apertures or to use artificial light. Artificial light adds contrast and detail to your photographs or movie footage. It also restores the colors that are filtered by water.

There are two types of artificial light used in still photography: flashbulbs and electronic flash. Each has its advantages; each has its disadvantages.

The initial cost of a flashbulb unit is less than that for an electronic flash. However, you will have the continuing cost of flashbulbs and, if

The Nikonos light meter and housing combination is inexpensive but reliable.
Courtesy Ehrenreich Photo-Optical Co.

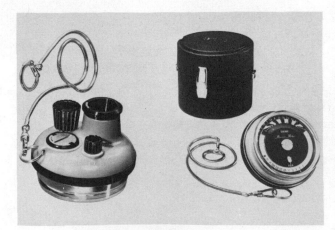

The Sekonic Marine Meter, designed especially for underwater photography uses a battery-powered cadmium sulfide cell to measure even very dim light.
Courtesy Sekonic Corporation

Using a Rolleimarin housing with its accessory flash gun, this photographer is equipped to take pictures having excellent color and contrast even at night.
Photo by Paul Tzimoulis, Skin Diver Magazine

you do a lot of flash photography, this can become a sizable amount. At relatively slow shutter speeds, say 1/60 second, a number 5 flashbulb (or its equivalent) is approximately three times as powerful as a 50-watt second electronic flash. The two types of flash have about the same power output at 1/250 second—the shutter speed required to freeze rapid action.

Electronic flash units eliminate the need to change flashbulbs. This is a significant advantage because flashbulbs are cumbersome to carry around under water and it takes time and concentration to change them. With an electronic flash, you will be able to freeze any type of action that can occur during a dive.

A few criteria for selecting either a flashbulb unit or an underwater electronic flash might help you in making your decision. If your budget for buying equipment is limited and if you plan to use flash infrequently—no more than about three dozen times a season—then you should choose a flashbulb unit. On the other hand, if your budget is not a prime consideration and if you plan to use flash fairly often, you should consider an electronic flash unit.

Artificial light for still photography can be used in two ways: either as total light or as fill-in light. Even in the bright subtropical waters, you might want to use fill-in flash techniques to restore the warm tones removed by the filtration of sunlight by water.

Both self-contained and surface-powered movie lights are available for underwater use. Both types employ tungsten filiaments and are color-balanced to match the characteristics of movie films designed to be used with artificial light. While the time duration of self-contained lights is usually very short (10 minutes or less), they allow you to operate independently of the surface. The short-time duration is not really a serious problem because most cameras have film capacities of even shorter durations. Self-contained underwater movie lights are relatively expensive because they require heavy-duty bat-

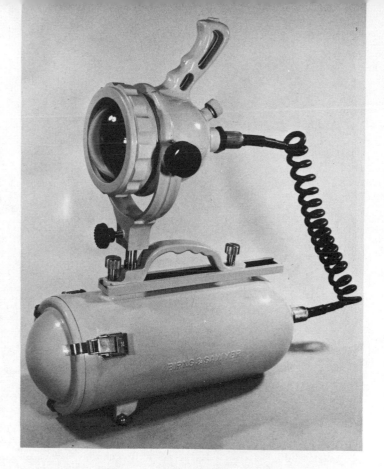

The powerful Birns & Sawyer movie light is used by many professional and U.S. Navy underwater photographers. It consists of a tungsten-halogen filament powered by nickel-cadmium batteries.
Courtesy Birns & Sawyer, Inc.

tery packs. They are also less powerful than surface-supplied lights because they must be powered by a battery pack that cannot be excessively heavy or bulky.

Films

Your choice of film for use under water will depend on your budget and the film format of the camera you intend to use. There are no special films for underwater photography; you must choose from the films available for your camera format. It is best to begin by using black and white film because the film processing costs are less than for color film. Black and white films are available in all the still-picture formats and for 16mm cameras. At present, they are not available for Super-8, and only in the major camera shops are they sometimes available in 8mm. Use color film only after you have acquired the ability

Use black and white films until you have gained proficiency. This photo was made with Tri-X film in the dark shadows of a coral ledge. The diver is purposely out of focus to place emphasis on the black angel fish.
Photo by Paul Tzimoulis, Skin Diver Magazine

to obtain consistently good black and white pictures or movies.

The film selection for cameras with fixed shutter speeds and fixed lens apertures is more limited than for adjustable cameras. Your choice in this case depends on the sunlight intensity, visibility, and depth. On clear, bright days when visibility is 25 feet or more, use Panatomic-X from the surface to 10 feet of depth; Verichrome Pan or Plus-X from 10 feet to 30 feet; or Tri-X below 30 feet. On a cloudy day when the visibility is 25 feet or more or on a clear, bright day when visibility is from 10 to 25 feet, use Verichrome Pan or Plus-X from the surface to 10 feet; Tri-X from 10 feet to 30 feet; or Royal-X below 30 feet. On a dim, cloudy day when the

visibility is 25 feet or more or on a cloudy day when the visibility is from 10 to 25 feet, use Tri-X from the surface to 10 feet and Royal-X from 10 feet to 30 feet.

Although all the films mentioned above are Eastman Kodak products, you can use other films of equivalent sensitivities. The Kodak films are mentioned simply because they are the most widely available and the most popular ones in the United States.

When you start using color film with your snapshot camera, you might try the following combinations. On a clear, bright day when the visibility is 25 feet or more, use Kodachrome II from the surface to about 5 feet of depth; Kodachrome-X or Ektachrome-X from 5 to 15 feet;

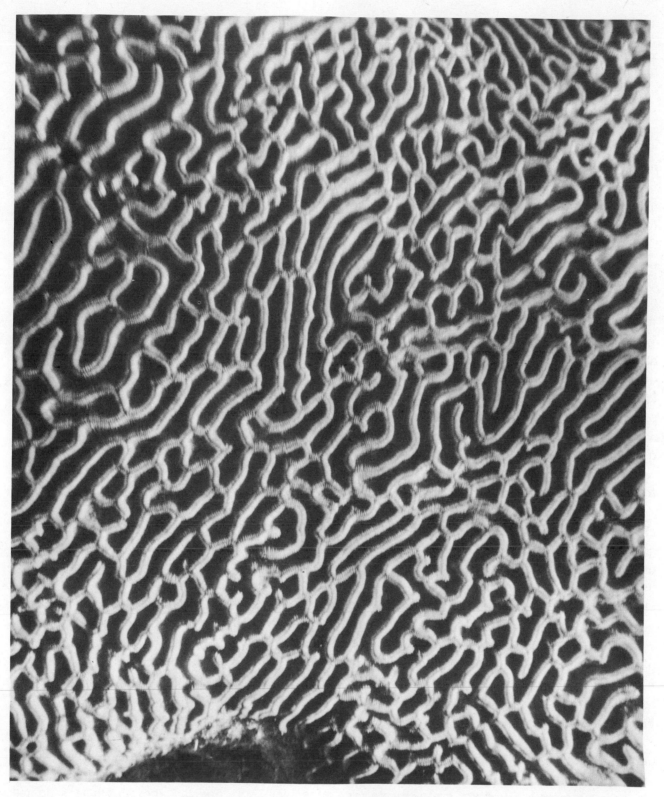

The abstraction was made by photographing brain coral at a distance of about 2 feet. A black and white print was obtained from a conversion negative of the original Ektachrome-X transparency.

Photo by Hank Frey

and High Speed Ektachrome from 15 feet to 30 feet. On a cloudy day when the visibility is 25 feet or more or on a clear bright day when the visibility is from 10 to 25 feet, use Kodachrome-X or Ektachrome-X from the surface to 5 feet and High Speed Ektachrome below that but to no more than 20 feet. On cloudy days when the visibility is from 10 to 25 feet, you will have to use High Speed Ektachrome from the surface to about 10 feet.

Your choice of film for adjustable cameras is considerably greater than it is for snapshot cameras. And, among the still-picture formats, there are more films available for 35mm cameras than for the other formats. Plus-X film offers great versatility in that you can use it both with available light and with artificial light during the same dive in most waters. A slower film, such as Panatomic-X is a better choice for close-up flash photography. It may be necessary to use Tri-X when the light level is low because of cloudiness, depth, or turbidity. Tri-X is also a good choice when you must use rapid shutter speeds to freeze the action.

In clear, bright, shallow water, try using Kodachrome II. Kodachrome-X, a faster film but with good color characteristics for available-light photography, should be used for depths greater than about 15 feet. Ektachrome-X is an alternate choice for cameras for which Kodachrome II is not available. High Speed Ektachrome is necessary when the available light is limited. For flash photography, Ektachrome-X is a good film for camera-to-subject distances up to about 6 or 7 feet. High Speed Ektachrome is more useful beyond this range.

The same film selection criteria apply for movies as well as for still pictures. However, your choice will be more limited because not all the films mentioned above are available for movie cameras. Many successful underwater photographers use Kodachrome II in shallow water regardless of the type of camera they have. Ektachrome MS (corresponding to Ekta-chrome-X) is a 16mm film that is useful for moderately limited light conditions. However, film processing costs are significantly higher than for Kodachrome II.

Flashbulbs

Your choice of flashbulbs depends on the type of shutter in your camera and on the type of bulb that fits your flash gun. Cameras with focal plane shutters require flashbulbs designed to synchronize with the shutter—FP bulbs. All other shutter types require bulbs designed for M synchronization. Your local camera dealer can advise you if you are not sure about the appropriate bulb for your camera.

Either blue bulbs or clear bulbs can be used for black and white flash photography at any camera-to-subject distance. For color photography, use blue bulbs for distances up to 7 feet and clear bulbs for greater distances. This will give good color balance in your photographs. Clear flashbulbs emit more red light than blue flash bulbs and therefore restore the warmer tones that are filtered by water.

The usual method for calculating the correct exposure in air is to use a guide number printed by the manufacturer on the flashbulb carton. Unfortunately, this guide number cannot be used under water without modification because water absorbs light at a greater rate than air. Correct the manufacturer's guide number by dividing it by 2.5. This will give you a guide number that can be used under water. For example, suppose the manufacturer's guide number is 200 for a particular film. Divide 200 by 2.5 to obtain an underwater guide number of 80. The guide number is the product of the distance times the lens opening. Therefore, the appropriate lens opening would be $f/22$ if the camera-to-subject distance is about 3½ feet; $f/16$ if the distance is 5 feet; $f/11$ if the distance is about 7½ feet; $f/8$ if the distance is 10 feet. The same correction fac-

Shaney Frey, at the mouth of a coral cave, was pho-
tographed using a number 5 blue bulb.
                              Photo by Hank Frey

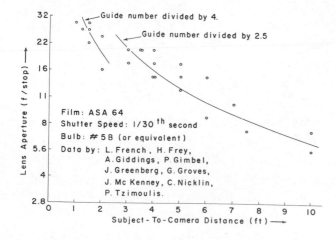

This graph, compiled by coauthor Hank Frey, shows
how the flash guide number correction was obtained.
                    Courtesy New York University

tor, 2.5, applies to electronic flash as well as to flashbulbs.

Filters

There is still a lot of controversy about the use of filters for underwater photography. You may have to do some experimenting on your own to determine whether or not you prefer to use filters or to shoot "bareback." Filters increase contrast and enhance color at the expense of using larger lens openings (or faster shutter speeds). They give your pictures whiter whites, blacker blacks, and greater distinction between colors.

*This pair of black angels was captured on film using
fill-in flash about 25 feet deep. Fill in flash increases
contrast and produces warmer tones in color work.*
Photo by Hank Frey

Filters alter light because they absorb some
of the colors and transmit others. This absorption requires the use of a larger lens opening
(or a faster shutter speed) than you would use
without the filter. You can use color-correcting
type of filters whether you use color film or black
and white film, or you can use yellow filters for
black and white film alone.

Coles Phinizy, senior editor at *Sports Illustrated*, has found that a combination of color-
correcting filters works best for available-light
color photography. In blue water, combine red
and yellow filters. A red filter and a magenta
filter combination is best for blue-green or yellow-green water. You can usually do without
filters from the surface to 5 feet of depth. Use a

CC10R and a CC05Y from 5 to 15 feet without
altering the lens opening. From 10 to 20 feet of
depth, use a CC20R and a CC05Y and open the
lens one-half *f*/stop. From about 15 to 25 feet,
use a CC30R plus a CC10Y and open the lens
one *f*/stop. From about 20 to 30 feet, use a
CC40R plus a CC10Y and open the lens one and
one-half *f*/stops. The overlap in the range of
depths will not affect your results significantly.
Substitute M (magenta) for Y (yellow) if the
water is blue-green or yellow-green.

A CC20R or a K1 (yellow) filter can be used
with black and white film from the surface to 30
feet of depth. You must open your lens one additional *f*/stop if you use either one of these filters.
From 20 feet to 70 feet, use a CC30R or a K2

This remarkable picture was made by using a red filter with black and white film to achieve maximum contrast.

Photo by David Doubilet, New York City

filter and open your lens one additional f/stop. A G filter should be used only in very turbid water with an additional lens opening of one and one-half f/stops.

All of the above applies to movie photography as well as to still photography.

Available-Light Techniques

The best time of day for available-light underwater photography is when the sun is highest overhead, usually from 10 A.M. to 2 P.M. The light level under water decreases very rapidly as the sun gets lower on the horizon. Mornings are often better than afternoons because the morning winds are usually not as strong as afternoon winds and surface waves reduce the light penetrating into the water.

Most beginners in underwater photography have trouble at first in obtaining good exposures. After some experience and consistently good exposures, you can turn your efforts to creative underwater photography. But first you must become a good technician.

You can increase the amount of light reaching the film in your camera either by opening the lens or by decreasing the shutter speed. Opening the lens one additional f/stop is equivalent to decreasing the shutter speed by one-half. For example, opening the lens from f/11 to f/8 is equivalent to changing the shutter speed from 1/125 second to 1/60 second. In the suggestions that follow, it will be recommended that you adjust the lens opening simply because this is usually the most convenient thing to do. However, you can choose to alter the shutter speed rather than to change the lens opening.

It is possible, though not preferable, to judge underwater exposures without using a light meter. You will find exposure information packaged with each roll of film. It will instruct you to use certain shutter speeds and lens openings for various sky conditions.

The ultimate in underwater photography, a Rebikoff Pegasus vehicle fully equipped with a movie camera and lights. This available-light picture was made 110 feet deep in the Mediterranean.
Photo by Ade Rebikoff, Fort Lauderdale, Florida

If you are shooting in a swimming pool, open the lens one additional f/stop wider than the manufacturer's recommendation. Use the same adjustment in open water if the bottom is light sand and no more than 10 feet deep. If the bottom is dark or greater than 10 feet deep, open two additional f/stops for depths to about 15 feet. Open one more f/stop for every additional 10 feet of depth greater than 15 feet.

A typical exposure for the Florida Keys or the Caribbean is f/8 at 1/60 second when using Ektachrome-X film or its equivalent at depths from about 10 to 25 feet.

If you use a light meter, hold it as close to your subject as possible to get a reading. Be sure that you read the light reflected from your subject and not the light from the water in the

Reduce the lens aperture by two f/stops to silhouette subjects against the surface. This scuba diver is unfouling a line off Santa Catalina Island.
Photo by Paul Tzimoulis, Skin Diver Magazine

distance. If you want to silhouette your subject against the surface by shooting from below, close your lens opening two f/stops.

Take most of your pictures or movies while shooting either horizontally or slightly upward toward the surface. Pictures taken from above the subject are usually confusing. Be very careful to hold your camera steady when you release the shutter or else the photograph will be blurred. If your camera has adjustable focusing, estimate the distance without regard for the fact that everything seems one-fourth closer in the water. It will "appear" closer to the film as well as to your eye. If you use a snapshot camera, do not try to take pictures closer than 4 feet from your subject or they will be out of focus. A good rule of thumb for limiting the maximum distance at which you take pictures is to divide the visibility by 4. For example, if the visibility is about 25 feet, limit your camera-to-subject distances to no more than about 6 feet.

There are numerous ways to frame good com-

Take care to hold your camera steady or your pictures will be blurred. Hank Frey steadies himself against the bottom off Los Coronodos Islands, Mexico.
Photo by Chuck Niklin, Diving Locker, San Diego, California

A prime example of artistic underwater photography. This photo was taken at 125 feet deep on "the wall" at Andros Island, Bahamas, during the early evening.
Photo by David Doubilet, New York City

positions. Many of them are inherent in the pictures used to illustrate this book. Some will be obvious to you.

It is important to have good cooperation between you and your model whenever you photograph people. Instruct your model to look your way frequently for hand signals and, when a scuba diver is posing for a picture, to exhale frequently. The shape and pattern of bubbles leaving a scuba regulator often complete the design of your picture composition. Your model's actions are even more critical when you are shooting movie film. Avoid photographing people from behind whenever possible because this angle can be unattractive. Head-on or broadside shots are usually better. Also, be sure that your model appears neat and without dangling harness straps.

The easiest objects to photograph are in the still-life category, including coral, plants, and animals that move very slowly, such as sea urchins, sea polyps, sea cucumbers. Abstract photographs can be created by shooting close-ups of coral, sea fans, sponges, and similar subjects.

Photographing fish is made easier if you learn their habits. Bottom-dwelling fish are usually found around rocks, sunken trees, coral reefs, and shipwrecks.

Flash Techniques

Brilliant colors are revealed where they are least expected by underwater flash, whether in clear tropical waters or in the more turbid northern waters. Used either as total or as fill-in light, the light from a flash makes it possible for you to produce a wide variety of underwater color spectaculars. Sometimes it is impossible to take pictures by the available light alone. Flash properly used permits you to take photographs regardless of depth or of time of day and provides far more contrast and detail in your pictures.

The most important technique in flash photography is to position your flash away from the lens. Hank Frey demonstrates this as he photographs the coral on Molasses Reef, Florida Keys.

Photo by Shaney Frey

The most important bit of advice is to position your flash gun away from the camera lens. Many commercially available flash guns have the flash reflector mounted about 18 inches away from the lens. This is all right for use in clear water, but it will not do for turbid-water photography. Light from a flash mounted too close to the lens is reflected directly back into the lens by the multitude of particles suspended in the water. Such flash bounce-back causes washed-out pictures.

Multiple reflections by many particles, called scattering, might ruin your picture when the flash is mounted near the camera or when the water is very turbid. As long as there are particles in the water, light will be scattered. You cannot prevent this. But you can minimize the damaging effect of scattering by positioning the

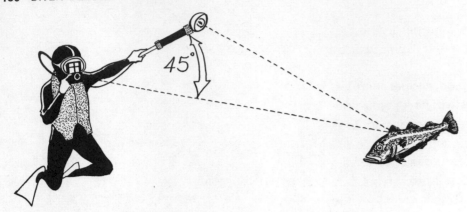

The basic hand-held flash technique.

flash reflector a minimum of 4 feet from the lens and by aiming the flash at a 45-degree angle. Light that is scattered by particles directly in front of the lens will be far less intense with the flash held in this manner than if it were only 18 inches away and directed straight toward the subject.

In addition to minimizing the unwanted scattered light, the extended flash decreases the total light path and, accordingly, provides greater illumination. The flash should be hand-held to achieve utmost versatility under different lighting conditions. In the beginning, you have to concentrate on aiming the flash correctly. It eventually becomes second nature—but you still have to be careful to prevent camera motion, because you hold the camera with only one hand. The technique may seem a little awkward at first, but it will become more and more comfortable —and it will certainly produce better pictures.

Choose the appropriate lens aperture after applying the guide number correction given previously in the section on flashbulbs.

There are a number of specific techniques for obtaining technically good photographs even under adverse conditions. First, you must limit your camera-to-subject distance to no more than one-fourth of the visibility. You will be safer if

you limit yourself to one-fifth of the visibility. By "visibility," we mean the distance at which you can no longer differentiate black from its surrounding environment in light of about dusk intensity. The visibility for white is considerably greater.

The extended flash is the basic component of the turbid-water flash-photography "recipe." You can get any photo with this scheme that you can get with a fixed gun—and more. Various effects are made possible by the versatile extended flash that cannot be obtained otherwise. And, in many cases, it means the difference between success and failure in turbid-water flash photography.

An effect that seldom fails to please is to frame your subject with an asymetrical shape in the foreground of the scene. Extend the flash beyond the foreground so that the frame itself remains dark. Illumination of the background subject with a darkened foreground strengthens the three-dimensional appearance of your photograph. Subjects for the foreground frame are a coral formation, sea fans, kelp, or a jagged section of a shipwreck. Almost any irregular shape will suffice.

Zone lighting is made possible by the extended flash gun. You can emphasize the pri-

Framing with the foreground.

Zone lighting the foreground.

Zone lighting the background.

Silhouetting with flash.

mary subject in your picture composition with this technique. A primary subject may be anywhere in your field of view, and it may be large or small as long as it becomes the most eye-attracting element in the picture. If it is in the background, raise the flash high and direct the light so that the foreground will be only weakly illuminated. To emphasize a foreground object, hold the flash almost directly over the object and point it downward. The background will then be subdued. It is sometimes possible to simulate natural sunlight by holding the flash directly overhead or at a slight angle.

Dramatic shots can be composed by silhouetting with flash. This is done by using a 10–20-foot extension cord or with a photoelectronically tripped slave flash. Many camera housings accept a double banana plug into their flash connectors. Common electrical "zip cord" and a few banana plugs may be all you need. Have a diver-model hold your flash with his back to your camera and the flash pointed directly away from you. This positioning will completely silhouette him against the background. Three-quarter and half-angle shots will also be effective. Just put the camera in his hand to make it

"Northeast Wreck," honored in the United States open competitions, was made with three flash guns —and cooperative helpers. One of the extension flashes is seen in this reproduction of the High Speed Ektachrome original.

Photo by Hank Frey

Close-up photography is possible even when the visibility is limited. This sea anemone was photographed in a lovely composition off Santa Barbara, California.

Photo by Al Giddings, Bamboo Reef of San Francisco

look as though he is taking a flash picture. Be sure that his flash is pointed toward an interesting object or the picture may look too contrived. You can use the light from his flash alone or you can fill in with a second flash. Be careful that you do not lose the effect by using too much fill-in light.

Two or more flash guns can be used to provide a wide variety of lighting conditions. Simply connect the additional units in parallel with your flash power pack. Set your shutter speed at 1/30 or slower because there will be a slight time delay between the flashing of the bulbs. Multi-flash techniques permit large-area and long-distance picture taking.

Close-up photography is the other extreme. Except for some difficulty in focusing, this is probably the simplest type of flash photography to do in turbid water. Even when there is only 8 feet of visibility, 1- or 2-foot camera-to-subject distances are possible.

Movie Techniques

Most of the principles for available-light still photography apply to movie photography as well. Framing your subject properly is more critical with movies than it is with stills. You can alter the composition of a still picture print by cropping it, but you cannot do this with movies.

Hank Frey pans a spadefish with his 16mm Bolex camera. Panning smoothly takes practice and concentration.

Photo by Shaney Frey

The advanced above-and-below technique developed by Coles Phinizy of Sports Illustrated results in dramatic shots such as this.

Photo by Coles Phinizy, New York City

Concentration and experience are required to achieve good framing.

Whenever possible, try to make your movie a complete story rather than a random sequence of scenes. The surest way to tell a complete and coherent story is to write a film script before the dive or at least to plan the movie before the dive. A script will help you to remember to shoot all the scenes needed for good continuity. A few brief topside scenes will establish where the underwater action is taking place and also show the models' faces.

You have a significant advantage over the land photographer in that you are able to move in all directions. However, you must remember to use smooth fluid motions whenever you expose footage while you are swimming.

If your camera is not equipped with an automatic exposure control, use either an exposure meter or the method for obtaining exposures without a meter described previously for available-light still photography.

Competition

There are more than a dozen underwater photography contests and festivals held throughout the year in the United States. You might wish to enter one or more of these contests after you have become a proficient underwater photographer. Be critical of your own work but do not hesitate to enter competition because you feel that your pictures or movies are less than flawless. Even if you decide not to enter your competition, you will undoubtedly learn more and benefit by attending the film festivals. Contact your local dive shop for information about underwater film contests and festivals in your area.

*There is a wide variety of hobbies to choose from—
including collecting underwater pets.*
     Photo by Paul Tzimoulis, Skin Diver Magazine

10 | Hobbies for Divers

When you begin diving in open water, you will find, as most tourists do, that you begin picking up souvenirs to show the folks at home—a bit of broken coral, a shell or two, or even a dried-up starfish to decorate your coffee table. You can do this in an unorganized and rather relaxed fashion, or you can organize your search for mementos and, in the process, develop a hobby.

You will probably start with the easiest item to collect—the seashell. Take a net bag to hold the specimens you collect. If the shell still contains a small animal, remove the animal completely and clean the shell by boiling it. Some shells are not really suitable for display, but if they are large enough and properly shaped, they can be cleaned and used to serve such dressed-up seafood dishes as clams au gratin and deviled crab.

Many shells are intricately conceived and attractive enough to merit being displayed imaginatively and individually. Scallop, amber pen, cockle, littleneck clam, tellin, angel wing, limpet, wentletrap, moon, horn, and many other fairly common shells are very handsome when cleaned and polished. Any one of these is a conversation piece when mounted on a well-proportioned carved-wood stand.

It may happen that most of the shells you come across will be run-of-the-mill shells—pretty, but not exceptional. But don't throw them back. They can be used to make a shell picture.

Shell Pictures

Look for small shells, pieces of broken coral, small starfish, sand dollars, loose pieces of sea fans, and the like when you dive. You can also usually find many shells washed up on the beach. Do not upset the natural balance of life under water by taking tools below to hack and pry rocks and coral loose. If you cannot pick it up in your hand, do not take it. Use a box to store these odds and ends. Then, when you have stored several dozen items, cut a sheet of sturdy cardboard from a carton or buy an inexpensive canvas panel at an art-supply store. You will also need picture-hanging wire (sold at art supply or hardware stores), a pair of pliers and a punching tool or glue and a glue brush, and a set of watercolors or oil paints.

Spread out your collection on a table and visualize how you can re-create either an actual underwater scene or, if you prefer, an imaginative design using the materials at hand.

Shell pictures are easy to do, yet they test your artistic ability.

Photo by Hank Frey

Paint the cardboard or canvas panel uniform blue or green. If you are artistically inclined, paint an underwater scene in soft, receding colors to give your final picture a three-dimensional effect. Lay the canvas flat on the table after the paint is dry. Experiment with your collection, placing and moving the shells and other pieces until you arrive at an attractive design or lifelike composition that satisfies you. Then you are ready to fix the pieces in place permanently.

In order to wire shells in place, you must make a hole on the underside of the shell and a corresponding hole in the canvas. Put the wire through the holes. Pull it through to the back of the canvas and twist the wire tightly. Other pieces such as coral, sea fans, and starfish can be wired inconspicuously without punching holes in them. If you wish to use glue instead of wire, use a strong, transparent glue following the directions given by the manufacturer. When

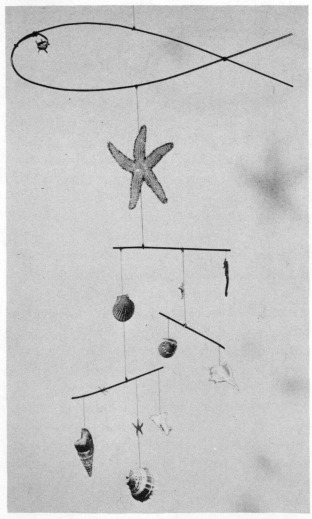

A mobile such as this can add the flavor of the sea to your den or recreation room.

Photo by Hank Frey

the picture is finished, frame it. A driftwood frame is a nice final touch for a shell picture.

Mobiles

Some divers enjoy making mobiles for their dens or recreation rooms. These are easily made and, with a little time and thought, can be very decorative. The same items used for shell pictures can be used for mobiles. The only additional materials needed are wire coat hangers or a length of heavy wire. Twist the heavy wire into the shape of a fish, seahorse, or ship; then decorate this basic shape with pieces from your collection box. Attach them to the central shape with varying lengths of wire until the mobile is delicately balanced so that it will move and turn as a mobile should.

Starfish Decorations

Starfish, because of their shape, lend themselves naturally to Christmas decorations. Holiday starfish can be used on wreaths for the door or windows and on the tree. If this idea appeals to you, all you have to do is collect starfish of various sizes. When you go diving, wear a pair of canvas gloves and carry a net bag. Just pick up the animals and put them in the bag. Let them dry

Starfish are simple to collect and to preserve. They lend themselves well to decorations.
Photo by Paul Tzimoulis, Skin Diver Magazine

Starfish are particularly suitable for making Christmas decorations. Note also the basket sponge filled with ornaments and artificial fruit.
Photo by Hank Frey

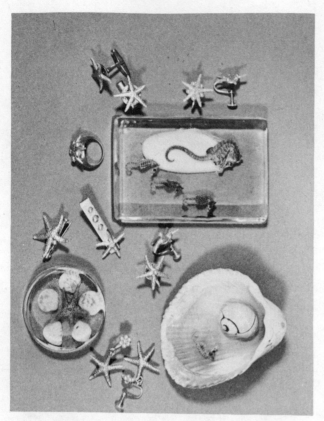

Tiny starfish and other specimens can be used to make earrings, cuff links, tie clasps, and decorative paper weights.

Photo by Hank Frey

Fish Prints

The next time you go spearfishing, take along a bottle of ink. Why? Because the fish you spear can pose—literally—for a work of art before it provides you with a tasty meal. You can make fish prints easily and quickly (speed, in fact, is important) with a minimum of art supplies. The process is a lot of fun. It can be done on the spot—on the boat, shore, or dock. And it can be a challenge to your imagination and creativity.

Fish printing, an ancient Japanese art form, will give you pleasingly attractive and delicate yet permanent records of your catch. You can create a striking jet-black print. Or you can use

A comely artist displays her work.

Photo by Hank Frey

in the sun for a day, soak them in 70 percent alcohol (30 percent water) for about one month, and then let them dry again.

There is practically no limit to the possibilities of decorating starfish. You can paint or spray the starfish bright colors. You can buy special glue and glitter at a hobby shop to really make them sparkle. You can even add large fake gems. A tree decorated with glittering starfish is uniquely beautiful when it is highlighted by tiny tree lights.

With Christmas or birthdays in mind, you might also want to try making gifts of jewelry with the tiniest specimens in your collection. You can make earrings, rings, tie clips, pins, and bracelets with glue and the basic jewelry pieces available at hobby shops.

several of numerous colors to approximate the actual natural coloring of the fish. The finished print will be a portrait that will show the complete profile of your fish—with each line in every fin and each scale, no matter how small, faithfully reproduced. Making fish prints requires no training or artistic ability. All you need is the inclination to try something old—but new in your experience—and a few inexpensive supplies, some of which can be obtained in most artist's supply stores:

Rice paper (large enough to cover the fish you hope to catch with at least 3 inches' excess on all four sides)

India ink—black, red, blue, yellow

Flat sable brush (about ½-inch)

Straight pins (found wherever sewing materials are sold)

Piece of cardboard or folded newspaper (large enough to hold the fish)

Some scraps of cardboard or newspaper

A few paper clips

Rice paper, a thin, almost transparent paper made from rice straw, is strong enough to absorb the moisture involved in the making of a fish print and is the most suitable paper to use. However, after you have had some experience with it, you may want to experiment with other materials.

Although India ink was not the original ink used by the Japanese, it works well and is a bit easier to use than the Japanese cake inks. If you wish to try the cake ink, it can be found at some Japanese shops and at some art supply stores.

The flat sable brush should be made of red sable, which is particularly soft and pliable. This softness and pliability means that you can brush your ink against the fish scales without lifting them up, thereby destroying the natural image.

After you have speared a decently scaly fish (fish with scales that are not prominent do not produce successful prints), put it on the cardboard or newspaper. Then prop the fins up level to the body surface by putting scraps of card-

Secure the fins in a fanned-out position using straight pins.

Photo by Hank Frey

Brush the ink on quickly, liberally, from tail to head.
Photo by Hank Frey

Press the rice paper firmly against the fish, rubbing your palm from tail to head—against the scales.
Photo by Hank Frey

board or newspaper beneath them. Fan out the fins—the dorsal, pectoral, and tail fins—and secure them in the fanned-out position with the straight pins.

Brush the ink on liberally and as quickly as you can. Brush from the tail toward the head *against* the scales. Leave the fins until last.

If you plan to use more than one color, use black first. If you use just one color, such as red, it will lose its intensity because it will be diluted by the natural moisture of the fish. The resulting print will be so pale that you will barely be able to see it. So use black first over the entire fish, then quickly apply one or more colors over the black ink.

Next, brush the ink carefully, though quickly, on the *spines* of all the fins. Try to avoid getting any ink at all on the tissue between the spines. This tends to cause a solid mass of color that completely obliterates the lovely natural design.

After you have applied your color or colors, carefully lay the rice paper over the fish. Center the fish under the paper. Then firmly press the paper against the fish. Rub the palm of your hand over the paper from *back* to *front* against the scales. Smooth the paper over the head.

Next, trace each spine of the fins with your fingers. All of this has to be done fairly quickly.

When you have finished making the print, lift the rice paper slowly, being very careful not to smudge the ink. Lay it on a flat surface to dry. It will dry after about five minutes. Roll it loosely and smoothly. Put a paper clip at each end of the roll and do not fold or crease the print in any way.

Your original intention when you speared the fish was to have it for supper. Wash the fish in fresh water until the waters runs clear. Then it can be cooked to your preference.

The really nice thing about fish prints is that you can make several prints from just one fish. After making one or two prints, you will be able to judge how much ink and speed you must use to get a successful print. After you finish a print, wipe the ink off the fish with a rag and start again.

If you make several prints, you can choose the best one for framing. It may happen that you have more than one print, perhaps two or more, that are good enough to be framed. In that case you might consider giving some of your prints as gifts.

Have the fish print framed at a shop or frame it yourself if you have the necessary materials on hand. It should be framed under glass just as you would frame a watercolor. The back of the print should be completely covered with heavy brown paper taped to the back of the frame. This will protect it from dust and dirt; fish prints cannot be cleaned the way oil paintings can.

The framed fish print is an unusual and beautiful addition to any home. It is truly the "art" of spearfishing.

Painting Under Water

Painting under water is an artistic endeavor suited to the scuba diver. Your air supply will last long enough because you will be sitting on the bottom in shallow water (about 15 feet deep)

A finished fish print.

Photo by Hank Frey

to get the most sunlight possible. The materials used for painting under water are the same as those used by a studio artist: a cotton canvas stretched on a wooden frame, a small table easel, a pallette, several painting knives, a small round brush, and oil paints. Tuck a few rags in your weight belt to clean the painting knives.

The first thing to do is to decide on a scene you want to paint. A level spot that gives you a good vantage point to work from is an important consideration. You need at least enough room so that you can kneel with the canvas in front of you and the pallette to one side. Have your buddy diver help you take your supplies down and weight them on the bottom. Drape a weight belt over the bottom portion of the easel (the easel itself holds the canvas in place) and put a weight right in the middle of the pallette. Anchor the painting knives and brush by simply shoving them into the sand. When your "studio" is all prepared, drape another weight belt over your legs and you are ready to begin. Your buddy can pose for you if you wish, but his most important contribution will be to serve as lookout and safety man. You will find that you become completely absorbed in your painting and someone must be alert to any danger.

Arrange the paints on the pallette before you take it below. Red and blue, green and crimson, violet and yellow, and a huge helping of white will give you any color combination you may want. Use one of the wax mediums in place of turpentine to mix colors on the pallette before applying them to the canvas. Use the one small round brush to block in your paintings and to put in small detail. Otherwise, use the painting knives and be sure to keep them clear as you go from one color to another. Do not try to do a finished painting in one sitting. You might have to return to the same location several consecutive days to complete it. Under most circumstances, you will only have one or two afternoons at the most, so you might have to do the finishing

Shaney Frey puts the finishing touches to an underwater oil painting. Painting under water is possible because oil paints and water do not mix.
Photo by Hank Frey

touches at home. It is a good idea to take a photograph of the scene to help you when you put in the final details.

If you would rather try a quicker and neater method of sketching under water, you can use wax pencils on an underwater slate to draw small subjects and transfer the drawing to a canvas later.

Whatever technique you use, never allow yourself to forget the rules of safe diving. Be prepared for a sudden surge of current that might sweep you off balance and for the tendency to drift away from the canvas now and again—perhaps to settle painfully on a silently waiting sea urchin. Be prepared, also, for tiny fish attempting to claim your pallette as their territory, nibbling at the piles of paint in the process. One thing may be safely said, no matter what the results of your painting efforts are, you are sure to have a new supply of amusing underwater tales to tell.

Salt Water Aquarium

It should be said at once that a salt water aquarium is much more difficult to prepare, to stock, and to maintain than a fresh water aquarium. It would take a full-length book to give you all the information required to embark successfully on such a project. (A good book on the subject by R. L. Straughan is listed in the bibliography.) All that will be attempted here is to give you the highlights.

It is possible to buy a salt water aquarium complete with fish, but that is an expensive undertaking and no challenge at all to you. Having decided to do it yourself, the first items on your list are the shells and coral that will both decorate the aquarium and provide shelter for the fish. The shells can be cleaned by boiling them. If any of the shells still contain animals, they must be removed before the shells are boiled. Coral must be soaked in fresh water for several weeks and the water must be changed every two days during the soaking.

The aquarium should be all glass or clear plastic that does not require any cement on any of the inside corners. To outfit the aquarium, you need a subsand filter and an air pump. All of this must be cured for several days by filling the aquarium with fresh water and adding three tablespoons of salt for each gallon of water. Then it must be emptied and rinsed with fresh water, filled with fresh water, and emptied again.

When all this is done, you can fill the aquarium with commercial sea water from an aquarium supply store or with sea water. After you turn on the pump and begin aerating the water, you can think about the fish it will house.

Collecting fish for your aquarium must be accomplished with care and consideration for the health of the fish. They cannot be handled to any large degree or they will sicken and die. Consideration must also be given to the kinds of fish that will be able to live compatibly—which means taking into account not only the species

but also the size and sex. The collecting can be done with a net or with a slurp gun.

When you start out to collect fish, take along some plastic bags, some rubber bands, and a portable foam plastic ice box (without ice). Collecting must be done quietly, patiently, and with little aggressive movement toward the fish. Hold the net so that it flows open with the current and try to allow the fish to move into it with the current. If this does not work, scoop up the fish as gently as possible. Keep the net under water while you transfer the fish into the plastic bag. Seal the top of the bag with a rubber band, leaving at least 4 inches of sea water for the fish to

Allow a large air space to remain in the collecting bag so that your fish will not suffocate.
Photo by Hank Frey

swim in and a large air space above the water. Put the plastic bag in the ice box so that the water will not become overheated and take the fish to its new, carefully prepared home.

A slurp gun can be used in place of a net, but it must be used with more caution. If a fish is literally slurped by the gun it will be injured and will probably die within a few days. This type of gun is used most extensively for collecting specimens for laboratory study when it does not matter whether or not they survive the collecting process. However, if it is used properly it can be harmless to the fish. Push the piston of the slurp gun forward to create a weak current. The fish will swim against the current just hard enough to remain stationary over the bottom. Then, stop the flow suddenly and the fish will enter into the barrel of your slurp gun. If the design of your slurp gun will allow it, pull the piston all the way back by hand. If not, pull the trigger. In this way, you should capture a fish without bruising it. Add some sea water to the plastic bag to bring the level up at least 4 inches before you "unslurp" the fish.

Artifacts

If your diving takes you to the sites of sunken ships, it is inevitable that sooner or later you will want to take something to prove that you have really been there. You cannot be blamed for that impulse. But you, and any other diver, can be blamed if, in the act of collecting, you succeed in destroying a home for underwater life. Fish need protection from their natural enemies. It is now general knowledge that wrecked ships quickly become a place of refuge for fish in places where shelter was not previously available. In attempts to increase the fish population to increase the food supply for us, artificial "reefs" in such forms as old cars, street cars, and concrete blocks have been deliberately placed on the sea floor.

So, if you want something to commemorate

Ferrous artifacts can be uncovered using a metal detector such as this one.
Photo by Paul Tzimoulis, Skin Diver Magazine

A veteran shipwreck explorer, Stan Levine, proudly displays an 80-pound bronze porthole recovered from the wreck of the Oregon. The 500-foot Cunard liner sank 14 miles off Jones Beach, Long Island, 79 years ago.
Photo by Paul Tzimoulis, Skin Diver Magazine

The dream of every treasure hunter! These pieces of eight and silver reales were discovered by treasure divers in Florida waters.
Photo by Paul Tzimoulis, Skin Diver Magazine

your dive, be sure that, in getting your souvenir, you destroy neither a source of food nor a shelter for fish.

For your own protection when collecting artifacts, it is best to wear heavy canvas gloves. Wrecks are often covered with sea anemones, which can sting, or with coral, which can cause painful cuts and scratches. Any artifacts that are worth displaying are worth the care needed to preserve them.

Metal objects that have been in the water for a long period of time are usually covered with a coral crust or some other sea growth. Remove the coating and boil the object in sodium hydroxide. Transfer it to an electrolytic bath using sodium hydroxide and zinc chips. Then soak it for several days in a solution of paraffin dissolved in xylene. When the object is removed from the solution, the xylene evaporates, leaving your souvenir permeated and coated by the paraffin, which protects it from the air and further corrosion.

Gold and pewter are not affected by long submersion in salt water and need only to be cleaned of any coating of sea growth.

Pottery, such as porcelain and partially vitrified or glasslike china, is not damaged by sea water and can be placed in a mild acid bath to remove any growths. However, old earthenware must be soaked in paraffin and xylene for several days to prevent it from crumbling.

Wood, bone, and leather completely disintegrate if not placed in successive baths of increasingly strong solutions of alcohol. Allow the object to drain and put it next into a xylene bath. Repeat the xylene bath once. Finally, soak the object in a xylene-paraffin solution to protect it from exposure to air.

Boating is a convenient and sometimes vital adjunct
to diving.

Courtesy Johnson Motors

Small power boats are by far the most suitable typ
for diving. Here, the young ladies act as tenders
divers exploring a wreck.

Courtesy Crestliner Raid

Many of the best diving spots are far beyond reasonable and safe swimming distance of shore-lines. Boating becomes a necessary adjunct to diving for offshore exploration of wrecks, coral reefs, and the waters that surround islands. There are many considerations worth making whether you plan to buy a boat for diving or to rent, borrow, or charter one.

Power boats are more suitable for diving than are sailboats because they usually have more usable cockpit and deck space. This does not mean that sailboats cannot be used; they can

Inflatable boats require no special launching facilities. They are easily launched from any type of beach.

Photo by Paul Tzimoulis, Skin Diver Magazine

be used, but not ideally, if a compromise must be made between love for diving and love for sailing.

There is no single ideal boat that will serve all purposes in all geographic regions. Any boat you select will have to be the best possible for the conditions under which the boat will be used. Among the criteria for selection are stability at anchor, seaworthiness, speed, trailerability, usable deck space, equipment-storage facilities, freeboard (height from the waterline to the gunwale), windshield and canopy (or a cabin), and your budget.

Small Craft

Many divers prefer boats small enough to be trailered conveniently to distant sites. Boats up to about 18 feet long with either outboard or inboard drives are well suited for trailering. Larger boats, say up to 25 feet long, can be trailered but with more difficulty and with more wear and tear on the transmission and read end of your car.

Inflatable boats eliminate the need for trailers and launching facilities. A well-manufactured inflatable boat is reliable, is durable, rides well, is fairly stable at anchor, and, like a tire, can withstand severe mechanical shock. The most serious criticism of the inflatable boat is that it is difficult to climb aboard because of the rather large, round, compliant pontoons. This problem can be minimized by using a properly weighted rope ladder and by installing hand grasps on the wooden decking. Rigid hulls are still much more popular despite the increasing trend toward using inflatables for diving.

A good diving boat must be a stable platform at anchor. It is difficult, if not dangerous, to work from a rolling round-bottom or V-bottom hull. Furthermore, these hulls tend to be tippy, and a sudden shift of a passenger's weight can send an unsuspecting and unready diver into the water

A good diving boat must be a stable platform at anchor. This Glasshopper tips very little with the weight of a scuba diver on its gunwhale.
Courtesy Johnson Motors

prematurely—or crashing onto the deck with a likelihood of injury. Diving from a rolling or tippy boat puts severe demands on agility and strength. Stability at anchor requires longitudinal flotation along the outer edges of the hull such as is found in inflatables, cathedral hulls, catamarans, trimarans, and similar but hybrid designs.

Seaworthiness is essential because bad weather and rough seas are not always predictable with great precision in all areas. A reliable self-bailer is important, as is the ability to maintain speed without shipping green water aboard and without severe slamming. Seaworthiness, however, is not a substitute for good seamanship. Small craft should always operate within

The Boston whaler is an excellent diving boat both under way and at anchor.
Photo by Paul Tzimoulis, Skin Diver Magazine

a safe distance offshore so that they can reach a haven quickly. Pontoon boats are poor performers while under way in rough seas. They are extremely stable at anchor and are excellent calm-water diving boats.

Adequate deck space is vital because divers need lots of room for suiting up and for donning gear. You will find few things more frustrating than going through acrobatic contortions in a crowded space to put on all the paraphernalia required for scuba diving. For this reason, the ideal diving boat has a maximum of clear deck space. Well-designed small boats often provide

more clear deck space than the larger luxury cabin cruisers. It would be better to suit up at least partially at the dock if you must use a boat with minimal deck space.

Good equipment-storage facilities are more than a convenience. Equipment strewn all over the deck and cockpit is hazardous and is subjected to damage. The design of storage facilities should take into account the need to store tanks, hardware, and rubber goods. It is preferable to secure tanks vertically to bulkheads (walls) using inelastic straps. Stored vertically, it is easy to attach the regulators to the tank

Pontoon boats provide extreme stability at anchor and a large, usable deck space.
Photo by Paul Tzimoulis, Skin Diver Magazine

Owen Lee, internationally celebrated diver, author, and photographer prepares to enter the water from the ladder of a pontoon boat.
Photo by Paul Tzimoulis, Skin Diver Magazine

valves without wrestling the tanks all over the deck. Inelastic straps are better than elastic ones because they will hold tanks firmly in place even when the boat rolls and pitches. Such items as camera housings, regulators, depth gauges, and compasses are relatively delicate pieces of hardware and should be stored in reasonably dry compartments designed to minimize shock and damage. At least one dry compartment should be provided for storing film and tank-pressure gauges. Such rugged hardware as weight belts and knives can be stored in wet areas that are conveniently accessible. Rubber goods, including wet suits, fins, snorkels, and masks, can be stored in wet areas or compartments. It is worthwhile to take the time to store such items in the sequence in which you will don them. Nearly constant housekeeping is required to keep gear from underfoot and to maintain some semblance of shipshapeness aboard small craft. Speared fish, lobsters, and "loot" from the bottom can be stored most conveniently in a live-bait tank or in a wet compartment that is easily washed with a hose later.

A cabin or a canopy is convenient for changing film in cameras and for protection against the hot sun or chilling winds.
Photo by Paul Tzimoulis, Skin Diver Magazine

This example of a good diving ladder makes boarding an easy task. It was placed on the transom to minimize tipping.

The freeboard height for a good diving boat is a compromise between ease of climbing aboard and having a dry boat. Low freeboards make boarding easier, but high freeboards reduce the amount of spray that can get into the boat. There is no simple rule of thumb for how high a freeboard should be. One in the vicinity of 15 to 30 inches high seems to be adequate for boats from 15 to 25 feet long.

The need for a windshield and canopy depends on the geographic area and on whether you will be operating in smooth water or offshore. In any case, a canopy is convenient for changing film because it provides the much-needed shade. Protection is desirable against the unrelenting hot sun in the subtropics and during the peak of the summer in the north. Shelter from chilling winds and cold spray is always welcome. The windshield on a diving boat will be used at times to steady a diver with all his gear and must therefore be built ruggedly. Walk-through windshields with hinged center sections make it easy to reach the foredeck.

A well-designed diving ladder facilitates boarding the boat even when you are encumbered with all your scuba gear. The commonly available swimmer's ladder meant for small boats not only is inadequate for divers but is unsafe. This type of ladder is simply put over the side and held with semicircular loops, but there is no pro-

The Century Trident has a built-in ramp and a water-tight bulkhead that separates the forward diving area from the main cockpit space. It is well equipped with storage spaces.

Photo by Paul Tzimoulis, Skin Diver Magazine

Boarding a small boat without a ladder is made easier if you remove your tank in the water.

Photo by George Field

A good ladder or ramp—or both—is a must when diving from large craft. These New Jersey wreck divers are getting ready to visit the remains of the Mohawk.

Courtesy Uniroyal Incorporated
and Donato Leo

vision for making it fast to the gunwale (upper edge of boat). It is difficult to get onto the ladder from the water because it does not extend far enough below the waterline. To make matters worse, the swimmer's ladder hangs close to the freeboard at an angle that requires you to lean backward and support your weight with your arms as well as with your feet. Even without fins, it is difficult to get a firm foothold on the rungs. A good diving ladder juts out at an angle of at least 20 degrees, has broad rungs, can be firmly secured to the gunwale, and extends at least 2 feet into the water.

Platforms and ramps are also handy, but unless they are incorporated into the design of a boat, they can interfere with the under way operation of the boat. A small boat with a low freeboard enables divers to climb aboard even without a ladder, platform, or ramp. To do this, remove your tank and weight belt and tie them onto a short length of rope secured to a cleat. Then, with the helping thrust of your fins, propel yourself upward and pull yourself over the gunwale. This requires strength and stamina, which invariably have diminished by the end of a dive.

Large Craft

Among the larger hulls, the sport-fisherman type is the most suitable for diving operations. It has lots of cockpit and deck space and a cabin large enough so that you can escape from the elements. Luxury cabin cruisers are perhaps the least suitable because they have a minimum of open cockpit and usable deck space. The sport fisherman and the cabin cruiser represent the two extremes; somewhere between the two are the various commercial hull designs including converted draggers, headboats, and utility boats.

Equipment storage is just as important with large craft as it is with smaller boats. Deck space can disappear quickly if three or more divers just strew their equipment around indiscriminantly. Provisions must be made for securing tanks in place and for stowing hardware and rubber goods.

Stability at anchor is less critical with large boats because they do not tend to tip as much as the smaller ones. There is, however, a critical aspect to diving from a large boat at anchor. It is usually more difficult and takes more time to weigh anchor. Divers surfacing some distance from the boat in a strong current may find it nearly impossible to swim to the boat. For this reason, it is safe practice to use a dinghy or other type of small boat. At the very least, an inner tube should be tied off at least 150 feet aft of the anchored boat.

A well-designed diving ladder is a must because the freeboard of large boats make it impossible to board them without a ladder. The general comments for ladder design applies to large boats as well.

Safe Practices

Boat handling and seamanship require study and practice. These skills can be learned by attending local Coast Guard Power Squadron meetings or by obtaining expert tutelage from experienced mariners. Beyond the normal knowledge of boat handling and seamanship, there are safety considerations that are peculiar to diving operations.

A sturdy length of chain will prevent your anchor line from being cut by sharp or abrasive objects on the bottom.

Photo by Hank Frey

The state of the sea surface may dictate that diving operations are unsafe. Weary, slightly incapacitated divers will find it both dangerous and difficult to board a ladder when the boat is rolling severely. At least one person should remain onboard to serve as an anchor watch. There have been incidences during which divers surfaced only to see their boats disappearing over the horizon—unattended. A sturdy length of chain is recommended at the anchor end of the line. Coral, jagged edges on shipwrecks, and sharp rocks have a particular ability to fray and part anchor lines.

The diver's flag should always be flown when divers are below—but only when divers are below. Conscientious diver-boatmen are justifiably intolerant of people who fly the diver's flag while they are under way.

When the diving crowd gets large, as it often

Diving from boats is great fun and it can open many new vistas. Good diving—and good boating!
Courtesy MFG Company

does on chartered boats, someone should keep track of who is in the water. In one fatal diving accident, the victim was not even missed until the charter boat had left the diving site! Diving from boats is great fun and it can open many new vistas—but safety and common sense must always be the first order of the day.

Good diving and good boating!

Appendix A: First Aid

Diving accidents generally happen in remote places where professional medical attention is not immediately accessible. As soon as possible, contact the nearest doctor, hospital, local or state police, or U.S. Coast Guard station. It is vitally important to apply first aid calmly and properly until help arrives. Your major concern should be to do no further harm. Analyze the situation as quickly and accurately as you can. Then act decisively. The three most important things to do are:

1. Give artificial respiration if the victim is not breathing.
2. Stop bleeding.
3. Treat shock.

Artificial respiration should begin within seconds after the victim stops breathing. This is the very first act of first aid to perform unless there is massive bleeding, which can result in death in just a few minutes. Moderate or minor bleeding can be attended to after artificial respiration has begun. Treatment for shock should begin as soon as possible.

The most serious or common situations requiring first aid are listed below with symptoms and recommended treatment. Carefully note that *not all symptoms may be present for a given accident*. This makes it difficult for a layman to perform an accurate diagnosis. In addition to diving accidents, wounds caused by the underwater environment and illnesses related to diving are covered.

DIVING ACCIDENTS

Drowning
Treatment:
Rescue victim swiftly, supporting him to prevent further inhalation of water.

Clear any obstructions in victim's airways by using your finger.

Begin artificial respiration quickly, during the rescue if possible (mouth-to-mouth or mouth-to-nose). See page 40.

Continue artificial respiration uninterrupted until victim recovers or is pronounced dead by a physician.

Send for medical aid.

Apply closed-chest cardiac massage if heart stops beating.

Remove victim's wet clothing and cover him with blankets or whatever is available.

Do not rub victim's limbs or apply heat.

Handle victim gently.

Air Embolism
Symptoms:
Bloody froth at the mouth
Staggering and dizziness
Confusion

Visual changes (such as blurred vision)
Paralysis, weakness, or tingling in the extremities
Collapse
Unconsciousness
Shock
Convulsions
Cessation of breathing

Treatment:

Immediate recompression in a chamber is required. If transportation is by air, use low-flying aircraft unless the cabin is fully pressurized.

Position the victim as shown in the illustration until he has been recompressed.

Apply artificial respiration if breathing ceases.
Keep victim warm and resting quietly.

Accidents Related to Air Embolism—Mediastinal and Subcutaneous Emphysema and Pneumothorax

Symptoms:

Mediastinal Emphysema

Pain under breast bone
Shortness of breath
Faintness
Blueness of skin, lips, or fingernails
Shock
Cessation of breathing

Subcutaneous Emphysema

Swollen (inflated) neck area
Skin crackles when moved
Voice changes
Difficulty in breathing and swallowing
Shock
Cessation of breathing

Pneumothorax

Sharp pain in chest (usually made worse by breathing deeply)
Shortness of breath, rapid and shallow breathing
Blueness of skin, lips, or fingernails
Shock
Cessation of breathing

Treatment:

Assume that victim also has an air embolism if he is unconscious or shows any one of the air embolism symptoms. See treatment for air embolism above.

Otherwise

Recompression is required for mediastinal or subcutaneous emphysema if breathing is difficult or if circulation is impaired.

Apply artificial respiration if breathing ceases.
Keep victim warm and resting quietly.

The Bends

Symptoms:

Local pain (usually leg or arm)
Tenderness, numbness, or pallor of overlying skin
Blotchy, mottled rash
Sensation of itching or burning
Dizziness
Loss of speech or hearing
Any visual disturbance
Extreme fatique and pain
Weakness or inability to use arms or legs
Shortness of breath
Chest pain (especially on inspiration)
Shock
Convulsions
Unconsciousness

Treatment:

Recompression is required. A physician may decide to forego recompression if only itches and rashes are in evidence. He may also decide to treat mild pains with aspirin, hot baths, and rest.

Keep victim warm with blankets, hot water bottles, hot soup or coffee.

Place victim flat on his back with his feet slightly elevated.

Anoxia, Carbon Dioxide Excess, Asphyxia

Symptoms:

Mental changes (similar to alcohol intoxication)
Poor responses, confusion, clumsiness, foolish behavior (anoxia and CO_2 excess)
Unconsciousness (muscular twitching with CO_2 excess)
Blueness (anoxia and asphyxia)

Labored breathing (CO_2 excess and asphyxia)

Headache, dizziness, weakness, nausea, sweating (CO_2 excess and asphyxia)

Breathing becomes violent, then stops (asphyxia)

Treatment:

Fresh air usually brings victim around.

Apply artificial respiration if breathing ceases.

Carbon Monoxide Poisoning

Symptoms:

Headache

Tightness across forehead

Weakness

Clumsiness

Nausea

Bad judgment

Dizziness

Confusion

Redness of lips, nailbeds, or skin

Unconsciousness

Cessation of breathing

Treatment:

Get victim to fresh air quickly.

Administer oxygen if it is available.

Apply artificial respiration if breathing ceases.

Cramps

Symptom:

Extreme local pain in leg or foot

Treatment:

Massage cramped muscles firmly. Apply heat if possible.

Electrocution

Symptoms:

Unconsciousness

Breathing stopped

Heart stopped

Treatment:

Do not touch victim before electrical current is turned off.

Get him to surface immediately

Begin artificial respiration if breathing has stopped.

Apply closed-chest cardiac massage if heart has stopped.

Face Mask Squeeze

Symptoms:

Pain

Bruised face

Bloodshot eyes

Treatment:

Apply cold packs to the injured area.

Medical care is required for serious injury.

Lung Squeeze

Symptoms:

Pressure on chest

Pain in chest

Breathing difficult on the surface

Bloody, frothy sputum

Treatment:

Place victim with head below body level to facilitate drainage if bloody, frothy sputum is present.

Seek medical aid at once.

Nitrogen Narcosis

Symptoms (while at depth):

No concern for own safety

Light-headedness

Increased (but false) self-confidence

Euphoria

Joviality

Dizziness

Reduced power of concentration

Delayed response

After severe narcosis

Amnesia

Sleepiness

Treatment:

None required unless profound depression or unconsciousness has occurred. If so, observation in a hospital is required.

Symptoms usually vanish as diver surfaces.

Ruptured Eardrum
Symptoms:

Severe pain in ear

Dizziness

Nausea

Temporary disorientation

Bleeding from ear

Coughing blood

Treatment:

Close outer ear passage with cotton to prevent contamination.

Consult a physician.

Shock (from any cause)
Symptoms:

Cold sweat

Pale complexion

Dizziness

Pulse feeble and rapid

Blueness of lips and fingernails

Shivering

Fainting or unconsciousness

Severe loss of blood (from wound)

Treatment:

Keep victim warm with blankets or whatever else is available.

Position victim with head downward and legs slightly elevated.

Give stimulants (except alcohol).

If victim is able to take fluids by mouth, mix one teaspoon salt with one-half teaspoon baking powder in one quart of water.

WOUNDS CAUSED BY THE UNDERWATER ENVIRONMENT

Bites: Shark, Barracuda, Moray Eel, Conger Eel
Symptoms:

Loss of body tissue (severe wounds)

Loss of blood (rapid loss with large wounds)

Shock

Unconsciousness

Treatment:

Pack wound with large gauze bandage and secure under pressure with elastic bandages.

Apply artificial respiration if breathing ceases.

Assume victim is in shock or will go into shock. Keep him as warm as possible.

Professional medical aid should be obtained as quickly as possible.

Bites: (Venomous) Sea Snake, Water Moccasin (Cottonmouth)
Symptoms:

Thickening of the tongue

Two puncture wounds or two pair of puncture wounds

Muscular stiffness

Pain

Weakness

Tightening of jaw muscles

Treatment:

Have victim lie prone and completely still.

Apply a tourniquet above the injury—on thigh for a leg wound and above elbow for an arm wound. Do not release the tourniquet.

Keep victim in prone position and transport him to hospital without delay.

Give accurate description of snake to attending physician.

Octopus Bite
Symptoms:

Stinging

Swelling

Redness

Bleeding

Treatment:

Apply antiseptic.

Control bleeding with pressure.

Recovery is generally uneventful. Seek medical aid if serious symptoms appear.

Bites or Lacerations: Groupers, Jewfish, Sea Turtles, Sea Lions, Etc.
Treatment:

Bleeding must be stopped with pressure bandages.

Apply antiseptic to ward off infection.

Keep victim warm.
Seek immediate medical care.

Venomous Sting: Cone Shell
Symptoms:
Local redness, swelling, and severe pain around the puncture wound
Sharp stinging or burning sensation
Numbness and tingling throughout the entire body (especially mouth and lips)
Paralysis
Unconsciousness
Heart failure

Treatment:
Apply closed-chest cardiac massage if heart stops.
Cleanse wound with cold salt water or with sterile water.
Soak in hot water for 30 to 60 minutes (not hot enough to cause burn).
Keep victim warm and resting.
Seek immediate medical aid.

Venomous Sting: Elkhorn Coral
Symptom:
Stinging or burning sensation

Treatment:
No specific treatment needed.

Venomous Sting: Fire Coral
Symptom:
Intense local pain
Redness and welts

Treatment:
Apply antiseptic to prevent infection.

Venomous Sting: Jellyfish, Portuguese Man-of-War
Symptoms:
Stinging sensation
Intense burning or throbbing pain
Stomach cramps
Nausea
Numbness
Swelling
Welts
Constriction of throat
Paralysis
Delirium
Convulsions

Treatment:
Quickly remove adhering tentacles with towel or sand (do not use bare hand).
Apply diluted ammonia or apply alcohol.
Seek medical aid at once for severe sting.

Venomous Sting: Sea Anemone
Symptoms:
Sharp, local pain
Possible redness with welts

Treatment:
No specific treatment.

Venomous Sting: Sea Urchin
Symptoms:
Intense local pain
Redness and swelling
Weakness
Paleness
Possible faintness

Treatment:
Remove as many spines as possible with tweezers.
Spines usually break off flush at wound surface and will dissolve in flesh.
Apply antiseptic and cover with loose bandage.
Seek medical aid at once if symptoms are severe.

Venomous Sting: Sting Ray
Symptoms:
Sharp, shooting or throbbing pain
Sweating
Vomiting
Swelling
Wound appears pale, then blue, then red

Treatment:

No specific treatment.

Clean wound and apply antiseptic.

Seek medical aid as soon as possible.

Venomous Spines: Catfish, Ratfish, Scorpion, Toadfish, Spiny Dogfish Shark

Symptoms:

Intense, throbbing pain

Redness

Swelling

Tenderness

Treatment:

Wound must be cleaned with cold salt water or sterile water.

Soak in hot water for 30 to 60 minutes.

Keep victim warm and resting.

Seek medical aid at once.

ILLNESSES RELATED TO DIVING

Dermititis

Symptoms:

Red rash

Welts

Severe itching

Inflamation

Splitting or peeling skin

Infection exuding fluid

Treatment:

Consult a doctor if rash does not respond to medicated powder or ointment or if infection develops.

Ear Infection

Symptoms:

Itching or pain in ears

Redness and swelling

Crusting

Exudation of fluid

Treatment:

Apply drops of diluted alcohol (3 parts alcohol to 7 parts water) to reduce itching and to dry ears.

Consult a physician.

Fish Poisoning (cooked fish)

Symptoms:

Stomach cramps

Nausea

Vomiting

Diarrhea

Weakness

Numbness and tingling sensation

Loss of coordination

Treatment:

Induce vomiting to purge stomach.

Keep victim prone, warm, and resting.

Seek immediate medical care.

Appendix B: Manufacturers and Distributors

The Anchor Shack
571 Jackson Street
Hayward, California

Aquala Sports Manufacturing Co.
Dept. T
P.O. Box 59218
Los Angeles, California

Bamboo Reef of San Francisco
584 4th Street
San Francisco, California

Dacor Corporation
5190 Church Street
Skokie, Illinois

Healthways
P.O. Box 45055
Los Angeles, California

Ikelite
3301 N. Illinois Street
Indianapolis, Indiana

Mako Products
2931 N.E. Second Avenue
Miami, Florida

New England Divers, Inc.
42 Water Street
Beverly, Massachusetts

Parkway Fabricators
348 Bordentown Avenue
South Amboy, New Jersey

Rubber Fabricators, Inc. (life vests)
Grantsville, West Virginia

Scubapro
17000 South Broadway
Gardena, California

Sportsways
Division of Pittman Rubber Co.
2050 Laura Avenue
Huntington Park, California

Underwater Sports of America
2945 N.E. Second Avenue
Miami, Florida

Seamless Rubber Company
New Haven, Connecticut

U.S. Divers Company
3233 West Larner Avenue
Santa Ana, California

White Stag Watersports Division
5203 S.E. Johnson Creek Boulevard
Portland, Oregon

W. J. Voit Rubber Company
3801 S. Harbor Boulevard
Santa Ana, California

Appendix C: U.S. Navy Air Decompression Tables
(reproduced from USN Diving Manual)

GENERAL INSTRUCTIONS FOR AIR DIVING

Need for Decompression

A quantity of nitrogen is taken up by the body during every dive. The amount absorbed depends upon the depth of the dive and the exposure (bottom) time. If the quantity of nitrogen dissolved in the body tissues exceeds a certain critical amount, the ascent must be delayed to allow the body tissue to remove the excess nitrogen. Decompression sickness results from failure to delay the ascent and to allow this process of gradual desaturation. A specified time at a specific depth for purposes of desaturation is called a decompression stop.

"No Decompression" Schedules

Dives that are not long or deep enough to require decompression stops are "no decompression" dives. Dives to 33 feet or less do not require decompression stops. As the depth increases, the allowable bottom time for "no decompression" dives decreases. Five minutes at 190 feet is the shortest and deepest "no decompression" schedule. These dives are all listed in the No Decompression Limits and Repetitive Group Designation Table for "No Decompression" Dives, ("No Decompression Table" (table 1-6)) and only require compliance with the 60 feet per minute rate of ascent.

Schedules That Require Decompression Stops

All dives beyond the limits of the "No Decompression Table" require decompression stops. These dives are listed in the Navy Standard Air Decompression Table (table 1-5). Comply exactly with instructions except as modified by surface decompression procedures.

Variations in Rate of Ascent

Ascend from all dives at the rate of 60 feet per minute.
In the event you exceed the 60 feet per minute rate:
(1) If no decompression stops are required, but the bottom time places you within 10 minutes of a schedule that does require decompression; stop at 10 feet for the time that you should have taken in ascent at 60 feet per minute.
(2) If decompression is required; stop 10 feet below the first listed decompression depth for the time that you should have taken in ascent at 60 feet per minute.
In the event you are unable to maintain the 60 feet per minute rate of ascent:
(1) If the delay was at or near the bottom; add to the bottom time, the additional time used in ascent. Decompress according to the requirements of the total bottom time. This is the safer procedure.
(2) If the delay was near the surface; increase the first stop by the difference between the time consumed in ascent and the time that should have been consumed at 60 feet per minute.

Repetitive Dive Procedure

A dive performed within 12 hours of surfacing from a previous dive is a repetitive dive. The period between dives is the surface interval. Excess nitrogen requires 12 hours to effectively be lost from the body. These tables are designed to protect the diver from the effects of this residual nitrogen. Allow a minimum surface interval of 10 minutes between all dives. Specific instructions are given for the use of each table in the following order:
(1) The "No Decompression Table" or the Navy Standard Air Decompression Table gives the repetitive group designation for all schedules which may precede a repetitive dive.
(2) The Surface Interval Credit Table gives credit for the desaturation occurring during the surface interval.
(3) The Repetitive Dive Timetable gives the number of minutes or residual nitrogen time to add to the actual bottom time of the repetitive dive in order to obtain decompression for the residual nitrogen.
(4) The "No Decompression Table" or the Navy Standard Air Decompression Table gives the decompression required for the repetitive dive.

U.S. NAVY STANDARD AIR DECOMPRESSION TABLE

INSTRUCTIONS FOR USE

Time of decompression stops in the table is in minutes.
Enter the table at the exact or the next greater depth than the maximum depth attained during the dive. Select the listed bottom time that is exactly equal to or is next greater than the bottom time of the dive. Maintain the diver's chest as close as possible to each decompression depth for the number of minutes listed. The rate of ascent between stops is not critical. Commence timing each stop on arrival at the decompression depth and resume ascent when the specified time has lapsed.
For example — a dive to 82 feet for 36 minutes. To determine the proper decompression procedure: The next greater depth listed in this table is 90 feet. The next greater bottom time listed opposite 90 feet is 40. Stop 7 minutes at 10 feet in accordance with the 90/40 schedule.
For example — a dive to 110 feet for 30 minutes. It is known that the depth did not exceed 110 feet. To determine the proper decompression schedule: The exact depth of 110 feet is listed. The exact bottom time of 30 minutes is listed opposite 110 feet. Decompress according to the 110/30 schedule unless the dive was particularly cold or arduous. In that case, go to the 110/40, the 120/30, or the 120/40 at your own discretion.   (Rev. 1958)

DEPTH (ft)	BOTTOM TIME (mins)	TIME TO FIRST STOP	DECOMPRESSION STOPS 50	40	30	20	10	TOTAL ASCENT TIME	REPET. GROUP
40	200						0	0.7	*
	210	0.5					2	2.5	N
	230	0.5					7	7.5	N
	250	0.5					11	11.5	O
	270	0.5					15	15.5	O
	300	0.5					19	19.5	Z
50	100						0	0.8	*
	110	0.7					3	3.7	L
	120	0.7					5	5.7	M
	140	0.7					10	10.7	M
	160	0.7					21	21.7	N
	180	0.7					29	29.7	O
	200	0.7					35	35.7	O
	220	0.7					40	40.7	Z
	240	0.7					47	47.7	Z
60	60						0	1.0	*
	70	0.8					2	2.8	K
	80	0.8					7	7.8	L
	100	0.8					14	14.8	M
	120	0.8					26	26.8	N
	140	0.8					39	39.8	O
	160	0.8					48	48.8	Z
	180	0.8					56	56.8	Z
	200	0.6				1	69	70.6	Z
70	50						0	1.2	*
	60	1.0					8	9.0	K
	70	1.0					14	15.0	L
	80	1.0					18	19.0	M
	90	1.0					23	24.0	N
	100	1.0					33	34.0	N
	110	0.8				2	41	43.8	O
	120	0.8				4	47	51.8	O
	130	0.8				6	52	58.8	O
	140	0.8				8	56	64.8	Z
	150	0.8				9	61	70.8	Z
	160	0.8				13	72	85.8	Z
	170	0.8				19	79	98.8	Z
80	40						0	1.3	*
	50	1.2					10	11.2	K
	60	1.2					17	18.2	L
	70	1.2					23	24.2	M
	80	1.0				2	31	34.0	N
	90	1.0				7	39	47.0	N
	100	1.0				11	46	58.0	O
	110	1.0				13	53	67.0	O
	120	1.0				17	56	74.0	Z
	130	1.0				19	63	83.0	Z
	140	1.0				26	69	96.0	Z
	150	1.0				32	77	110.0	Z
90	30						0	1.5	*
	40	1.3					7	8.3	J
	50	1.3					18	19.3	L
	60	1.3					25	26.3	M
	70	1.2				7	30	38.2	N
	80	1.2				13	40	54.2	N
	90	1.2				18	48	67.2	O
	100	1.2				21	54	76.2	Z
	110	1.2				24	61	86.2	Z
	120	1.2				32	68	101.2	Z
	130	1.0			5	36	74	116.0	Z
100	25						0	1.7	*
	30	1.5					3	4.5	I
	40	1.5					15	16.5	K
	50	1.3				2	24	27.3	L
	60	1.3				9	28	38.3	N
	70	1.3				17	39	57.3	O
	80	1.3				23	48	72.3	O
	90	1.2			3	23	57	84.2	Z
	100	1.2			7	23	66	97.2	Z
	110	1.2			10	34	72	117.2	Z
	120	1.2			12	41	78	132.2	Z
110	20						0	1.8	*
	25	1.7					3	4.7	H
	30	1.7					7	8.7	J
	40	1.5				2	21	24.5	L
	50	1.5				8	26	35.5	M
	60	1.5				18	36	55.5	N
	70	1.3			1	23	48	73.3	O
	80	1.3			7	23	57	88.3	Z
	90	1.3			12	30	64	107.3	Z
	100	1.3			15	37	72	125.3	Z

DEPTH (ft)	BOTTOM TIME (mins)	TIME TO FIRST STOP	DECOMPRESSION STOPS 50	40	30	20	10	TOTAL ASCENT TIME	REPET. GROUP
120	15						0	2.0	*
	20	1.8					2	3.8	H
	25	1.8					6	7.8	I
	30	1.8					14	15.8	J
	40	1.7				5	25	31.7	L
	50	1.7				15	31	47.7	N
	60	1.5			2	22	45	70.5	O
	70	1.5			9	23	55	88.5	O
	80	1.5			15	27	63	106.5	Z
	90	1.5			19	37	74	131.5	Z
	100	1.5			23	45	80	149.5	Z
130	10						0	2.2	*
	15	2.0					1	3.0	F
	20	2.0					4	6.0	H
	25	2.0					10	12.0	J
	30	1.8			3	18		22.8	M
	40	1.8			10	25		36.8	N
	50	1.7			3	21	37	62.7	O
	60	1.7			9	23	52	85.7	Z
	70	1.7			16	24	61	102.7	Z
	80	1.5		3	19	35	72	130.5	Z
	90	1.5		8	19	45	80	153.5	Z
140	10						0	2.3	*
	15	2.2					2	4.2	G
	20	2.2					6	8.2	I
	25	2.0			2	14		18.0	J
	30	2.0			5	21		28.0	K
	40	1.8		2	16	26		45.8	N
	50	1.8		6	24	44		75.8	O
	60	1.8		16	23	56		96.8	Z
	70	1.7		4	19	32	68	124.7	Z
	80	1.7		10	23	41	79	154.7	Z
150	5						0	2.5	C
	10	2.3					1	3.3	E
	15	2.3					3	5.3	G
	20	2.2				7		11.2	H
	25	2.2			4	17		23.2	K
	30	2.2			8	24		34.2	L
	40	2.0		5	19	33		59.0	N
	50	2.0		12	23	51		88.0	O
	60	1.8	3	19	26	62		111.8	Z
	70	1.8	11	19	39	75		145.8	Z
	80	1.7	1	17	19	50	84	172.7	Z
160	5						0	2.7	D
	10	2.5					1	3.5	F
	15	2.3			1	4		7.3	H
	20	2.3			3	11		16.3	J
	25	2.3			7	20		29.3	K
	30	2.2		2	11	25		40.2	M
	40	2.2		7	23	39		71.2	N
	50	2.0	2	16	23	55		98.0	Z
	60	2.0	9	19	33	69		132.0	Z
	70	1.8	1	17	22	44	80	165.8	Z
170	5						0	2.8	D
	10	2.7					2	4.7	F
	15	2.5				2	5	9.5	H
	20	2.5				4	15	21.5	J
	25	2.3			2	7	23	34.3	L
	30	2.3			4	13	26	45.3	M
	40	2.2		1	10	23	45	81.2	O
	50	2.2		5	18	23	61	109.2	Z
	60	2·0	2	15	22	37	74	152.0	Z
	70	2.0	8	17	19	51	86	183.0	Z
180	5						0	3.0	D
	10	2.8					3	5.8	F
	15	2.7				3	6	11.7	I
	20	2.5			1	5	17	25.5	K
	25	2.5			3	10	24	39.5	L
	30	2.5			6	17	27	52.5	N
	40	2.3		3	14	23	50	92.3	O
	50	2.2	2	9	19	30	65	127.2	Z
	60	2.2	5	16	19	44	81	167.2	Z
190	5						0	3.2	D
	10	2.8				1	3	6.8	G
	15	2.8				4	7	13.8	I
	20	2.7			2	6	20	30.7	K
	25	2.7			5	11	25	43.7	M
	30	2.5		1	8	19	32	62.5	N
	40	2.5		8	14	23	55	102.5	O
	50	2.3	4	13	22	33	72	146.3	Z
	60	2.3	10	17	19	50	84	182.3	Z

Note: Depths below 130' are not recommended for sports diving.

*See table on following page for repetitive groups as in "no decompression" dives.

DEPTH (ft.)	NO DECOMPRESSION LIMITS (Min.)	REPETITIVE GROUPS														
		A	B	C	D	E	F	G	H	I	J	K	L	M	N	O
10	–	60	120	210	300											
15	–	35	70	110	160	225	350									
20	–	25	50	75	100	135	180	240	325							
25	–	20	35	55	75	100	125	160	195	245	315					
30	–	15	30	45	60	75	95	120	145	170	205	250	310			
35	310	5	15	25	40	50	60	80	100	120	140	160	190	220	270	310
40	200	5	15	25	30	40	50	70	80	100	110	130	150	170	200	
50	100	–	10	15	25	30	40	50	60	70	80	90	100			
60	60	–	10	15	20	25	30	40	50	55	60					
70	50	–	5	10	15	20	30	35	40	45	50					
80	40	–	5	10	15	20	25	30	35	40						
90	30	–	5	10	12	15	20	25	30							
100	25	–	5	7	10	15	20	22	25							
110	20	–	–	5	10	13	15	20								
120	15	–	–	5	10	12	15									
130	10	–	–	5	8	10										
140	10	–	–	5	7	10										
150	5	–	–	5												
160	5	–	–	–	5											
170	5	–	–	–	5											
180	5	–	–	–	5											
190	5	–	–	–	5											

(Rev. 1958)

INSTRUCTIONS FOR USE

I. "No decompression" limits

This column shows at various depths greater than 30 feet the allowable diving times (in minutes) which permit surfacing directly at 60 ft. a minute with no decompression stops. Longer exposure times require the use of the Standard Air Decompression Table (Table 1-5).

II. Repetitive group designation table

The tabulated exposure times (or bottom times) are in minutes. The times at the various depths in each vertical column are the maximum exposures during which a diver will remain within the group listed at the head of the column.

To find the repetitive group designation at surfacing for dives involving exposures up to and including the "no decompression limits": Enter the table on the exact or next greater depth than that to which exposed and select the listed exposure time exact or next greater than the actual exposure time. The repetitive group designation is indicated by the letter at the head of the vertical column where the selected exposure time is listed.

For example: A dive was to 32 feet for 45 minutes. Enter the table along the 35 ft. depth line since it is next greater than 32 ft. The table shows that since group "D" is left after 40 minutes exposure and group "E" after 50 minutes, group "E" (at the head of the column where the 50 min. exposure is listed) is the proper selection.

Exposure times for depths less than 40 ft. are listed only up to approximately five hours since this is considered to be beyond field requirements for this table.

Note: Depths below 130' are not recommended for sports diving.

REPETITIVE GROUP AT THE END OF THE SURFACE INTERVAL

	Z	O	N	M	L	K	J	I	H	G	F	E	D	C	B	A
Z	0:10-0:22	0:34	0:48	1:02	1:18	1:36	1:55	2:17	2:42	3:10	3:45	4:29	5:27	6:56	10:05	12:00*
O		0:10-0:23	0:36	0:51	1:07	1:24	1:43	2:04	2:29	2:59	3:33	4:17	5:16	6:44	9:54	12:00*
N			0:10-0:24	0:39	0:54	1:11	1:30	1:53	2:18	2:47	3:22	4:04	5:03	6:32	9:43	12:00*
M				0:10-0:25	0:42	0:59	1:18	1:39	2:05	2:34	3:08	3:52	4:49	6:18	9:28	12:00*
L					0:10-0:26	0:45	1:04	1:25	1:49	2:19	2:53	3:36	4:35	6:02	9:12	12:00*
K						0:10-0:28	0:49	1:11	1:35	2:03	2:38	3:21	4:19	5:48	8:58	12:00*
J							0:10-0:31	0:54	1:19	1:47	2:20	3:04	4:02	5:40	8:40	12:00*
I								0:10-0:33	0:59	1:29	2:02	2:44	3:43	5:12	8:21	12:00*
H									0:10-0:36	1:06	1:41	2:23	3:20	4:49	7:59	12:00*
G										0:10-0:40	1:15	1:59	2:58	4:25	7:35	12:00*
F											0:10-0:45	1:29	2:28	3:57	7:05	12:00*
E												0:10-0:54	1:57	3:22	6:32	12:00*
D													0:10-1:09	2:38	5:48	12:00*
C														0:10-1:39	2:49	12:00*
B															0:10-2:10	12:00*
A																0:10-12:00*

REPETITIVE GROUP AT THE BEGINNING OF SURFACE INTERVAL (FROM PREVIOUS DIVE)

(Rev. 1958)

INSTRUCTIONS FOR USE

Surface interval time in the table is in hours and minutes ("7:59" means 7 hours and 59 minutes). The surface interval must be at least 10 minutes.

Find the repetitive group designation letter (from the previous dive schedule) on the diagonal slope. Enter the table horizontally to select the listed surface interval time that is exactly or next greater than the actual surface interval time. The repetitive group designation for the end of the surface interval is at the head of the vertical column where the selected surface interval time is listed. For example — a previous dive was to 110 ft. for 30 minutes. The diver remains on the surface 1 hour and 30 minutes and wishes to find the new repetitive group designation: The repetitive group from the last column of the 110/30 schedule in the Standard Air Decompression Tables is "J". Enter the surface interval credit table along the horizontal line labeled "J". The 1 hour and 47 min. listed surface interval time is next greater than the actual 1 hour and 30 minutes surface interval time. Therefore, the diver has lost sufficient inert gas to place him in group "G" (at the head of the vertical column selected).

*NOTE: Dives following surface intervals of more than 12 hours are not considered repetitive dives. Actual bottom times in the Standard Air Decompression Tables may be used in computing decompression for such dives.

REPET. GROUPS	REPETITIVE DIVE DEPTH (Ft.)															
	40	50	60	70	80	90	100	110	120	130	140	150	160	170	180	190
A	7	6	5	4	4	3	3	3	3	3	2	2	2	2	2	2
B	17	13	11	9	8	7	7	6	6	6	5	5	4	4	4	4
C	25	21	17	15	13	11	10	10	9	8	7	7	6	6	6	6
D	37	29	24	20	18	16	14	13	12	11	10	9	9	8	8	8
E	49	38	30	26	23	20	18	16	15	13	12	12	11	10	10	10
F	61	47	36	31	28	24	22	20	18	16	15	14	13	13	12	11
G	73	56	44	37	32	29	26	24	21	19	18	17	16	15	14	13
H	87	66	52	43	38	33	30	27	25	22	20	19	18	17	16	15
I	101	76	61	50	43	38	34	31	28	25	23	22	20	19	18	17
J	116	87	70	57	48	43	38	34	32	28	26	24	23	22	20	19
K	138	99	79	64	54	47	43	38	35	31	29	27	26	24	22	21
L	161	111	88	72	61	53	48	42	39	35	32	30	28	26	25	24
M	187	124	97	80	68	58	52	47	43	38	35	32	31	29	27	26
N	213	142	107	87	73	64	57	51	46	40	38	35	33	31	29	28
O	241	160	117	96	80	70	62	55	50	44	40	38	36	34	31	30
Z	257	169	122	100	84	73	64	57	52	46	42	40	37	35	32	31

(Rev. 1958)

INSTRUCTIONS FOR USE

The bottom times listed in this table are called "residual nitrogen times" and are the times a diver is to consider he has already spent on bottom when he starts a repetitive dive to a specific depth. They are in minutes.

Enter the table horizontally with the repetitive group designation from the Surface Interval Credit Table. The time in each vertical column is the number of minutes that would be required (at the depth listed at the head of the column) to saturate to the particular group.

For example — the final group designation from the Surface Interval Credit Table, on the basis of a previous dive and surface interval, is "H". To plan a dive to 110 feet, determine the "residual nitrogen time" for this depth required by the repetitive group designation: Enter this table along the horizontal line labeled "H". The table shows that one must start a dive to 110 feet as though he had already been on the bottom for 27 minutes. This information can then be applied to the Standard Air Decompression table or "No Decompression" Table in a number of ways:

(1) Assuming a diver is going to finish a job and take whatever decompression is required, he must add 27 minutes to his actual bottom time and be prepared to take decompression according to the 110 foot schedules for the sum or equivalent single dive time.

(2) Assuming one wishes to make a quick inspection dive for the minimum decompression, he will decompress according to the 110/30 schedule for a dive of 3 minutes or less (27 + 3 = 30). For a dive of over 3 minutes but less than 13, he will decompress according to the 110/40 schedule (27 + 13 = 40).

(3) Assuming that one does not want to exceed the 110/50 schedule and the amount of decompression it requires, he will have to start ascent before 23 minutes of actual bottom time (50 - 27 = 23).

(4) Assuming that a diver has air for approximately 45 minutes bottom time and decompression stops, the possible dives can be computed: A dive of 13 minutes will require 23 minutes of decompression (110/40 schedule), for a total submerged time of 36 minutes. A dive of 13 to 23 minutes will require 34 minutes of decompression (110/50 schedule), for a total submerged time of 47 to 57 minutes. Therefore, to be safe, the diver will have to start ascent before 13 minutes or a standby air source will have to be provided.

Note: Depths below 130' are not recommended for sports diving.

REPETITIVE DIVE WORKSHEET

I. PREVIOUS DIVE:

___ minutes ⎱ see table 1-5 or 1-6 for

____ feet   ⎰ repetitive group designation ⎱ Group___

II. SURFACE INTERVAL:

__hours__minutes on surface ⎱ see table 1-7

Group___ (from I.) ⎰ for new group ⎱ Group___

III. RESIDUAL NITROGEN TIME:

____ feet (depth of repetitive dive) ⎱ see table

Group___ (from II.) ⎰ 1-8 ⎱ __minutes

IV. EQUIVALENT SINGLE DIVE TIME:

___ minutes (residual nitrogen time from III.)

(add) ___ minutes (actual bottom time of repetitive dive)

(sum) ___ minutes

V. DECOMPRESSION FOR REPETITIVE DIVE:

___ minutes (equivalent single dive ⎱ see table
          time from IV.)
____ feet (depth of repetitive dive) ⎰ 1-5 or 1-6

☐ No decompression required
or
Decompression stops:____ feet____minutes

____feet____minutes

____feet____minutes

____feet____minutes

Bibliography

Barada, B. "The Ideal Skin Diving Boat," *Skin Diver Magazine* (July 1965).

——. "What Is a Dive Boat?" *Skin Diver Magazine* (March 1968).

Christiansen, J. "Spearfishing Tips," *Dive* (February 1968).

Council for National Cooperation in Aquatics. *The New Science of Skin and Scuba Diving.* New York: Association Press, 1966.

Frey, H. "A Complete Underwater Flash System," *Skin Diver Magazine* (June 1965).

——. "Turbid Water Flash Photography," *Skin Diver Magazine* (July 1965).

——. "Flash Guide Numbers for Subsea Shooting," *Skin Diver Magazine* (September 1967).

——. "Thermal Protection," *Skin Diver Magazine* (October–November 1967).

——. "Underwater Movie Lights," *Skin Diver Magazine* (January 1968).

——, and S. Frey. *130 Feet Down—Handbook for Hydronauts.* New York: Harcourt, Brace & World, 1961.

——, and P. Tzimoulis. *Camera Below—The Complete Guide to the Art and Science of Underwater Photography.* New York: Association Press, 1968.

Frey, S. *The Complete Beginner's Guide to Skin Diving.* New York: Doubleday, 1965.

Gilbert, P. W. (Ed.). *Sharks and Survival.* Boston: Heath, 1963.

Halstead, B. W., M.D. *Dangerous Marine Animals.* Cambridge, Cornell Maritime Press, 1959.

Lambertsen, C. J., M.D., and L. J. Greenbaum, M.D. (Eds.). *Second Symposium on Underwater Physiology.* Publication 1181. Washington, D.C.: National Academy of Sciences—National Research Council, 1963.

Miles, S. *Underwater Medicine.* Second Ed. Philadelphia: Lippincott, 1966.

Morgan, B. "Focus On Regulators," *Skin Diver Magazine* (June 1963).

Phinizy, C. Personal communications, 1966-8.

Ray, C., and E. Ciampi. *The Underwater Guide to Marine Life.* New York: Barnes, 1956.

Schuch, John and Joe (Cougar Sports, Bronx, N.Y.). Personal communications, 1967-8.

Straughan, R. L. *The Salt-Water Aquarium in the Home.* New York: Barnes, 1959.

Submarine Medicine Practice. Bureau of Medicine and Surgery, NAVMED-P 5054. Washington, D.C.: Government Printing Office, 1956.

U.S. Navy Diving Manual. NAVSHIPS 250-538. Washington, D.C.: Government Printing Office, 1959.

Index